FURNISHING PLAN
FOR A
BADLANDS RANCH HOUSE

THEOD'RE ROOSEVELT
NATIONAL MEMORIAL PARK

NORTH DAKOTA

by
Lenard E. Brown

DIVISION OF HISTORY

OFFICE OF ARCHEOLOGY AND HISTORIC PRESERVATION

OCTOBER 31, 1969

U.S. DEPARTMENT OF THE INTERIOR   NATIONAL PARK SERVICE

FOREWORD

This discussion of typical furnishings in ranch houses of western Dakota or eastern Montana during the last two decades of the nineteenth century was completed to fulfill the requirements of RSP H-1 from Theodore Roosevelt National Memorial Park. This unit of the National Park System on the western edge of North Dakota honors the activities of Theodore Roosevelt in that part of the west between 1883 and 1899. Roosevelt's active involvement in Dakota ranching lasted less than five years, but he visited his Elkhorn Ranch nearly every autumn on hunting trips. Roosevelt last saw the land where "the romance of my life began" in 1903.

The spell of the North Dakota Badlands along the Little Missouri caught Roosevelt during his first extended stay in the region. In June of 1884 he wrote his sister, Anna, and on two occasions talked of the land:[1]

> The country is growing on me, more and more; it has a curious fantastic beauty of its own; and as I own six or eight horses I have a fresh one every day and ride on a lope all day long . . . . There is not much game however; the cattlemen have cleaned it out and only a few antelope and deer remain. [Letter of June 17, 1884]

=====

1. Both of the quotes that follow are from Anna R. Cowles, *Letters from Theodore Roosevelt to Anna Roosevelt Cowles, 1870-1918* (New York, 1924), p. 58-59. This same enthusiasm surfaces in Roosevelt's writings on his life in the West: *Hunting Trips of a Ranchman, Ranch Life and the Hunting Trail, The Wilderness Hunter,* and his *Autobiography.*

The country has widely different aspects in
different places; one day I will canter hour after
hour over the level green grass, or through miles of
wild rose thickets, all in bloom; on the next I would
be amid the savage desolation of the Bad Lands with
their dreary plateaus, fantastically shaped buttes
and deep winding canyons. I enjoyed the trip greatly
and have never been in better health. [June 23, 1884]

The spell remains strong today. John Steinbeck, one of the

giants of American literature, described his feelings as he

approached the rugged country from the east and during a brief

stop in the badlands:

As I was not prepared for the Missouri [River]
boundary, so I was not prepared for the Bad Lands.
They deserve this name. They are like the work of an
evil child. Such a place the Fallen Angels might have
built as a spite to Heaven, dry and sharp, desolate
and dangerous, and for me filled with foreboding. A
sense comes from it that it does not like or welcome
humans. But humans being what they are, and I being
human, I turned off the highway on a shaley road and
headed in among the buttes, but with a shyness as though
I crashed a party. . . . What a place for a colony of
troglodytes or better, trolls. And here is an odd
thing. Just as I felt unwanted in this land, so do I
feel a reluctance in writing about it.

        *   *   *   *   *   *

I went into a state of flight, running to getaway from
the unearthly landscape. And then the late afternoon
changed everything. As the sun angled, the buttes and
coulees, the cliffs and sculptured hills and ravines
lost their burned and dreadful look and glowed with
yellow and rich browns and a hundred variations of red
and silver gray, all picked out by streaks of coal black.
It was so beautiful that I stopped near a thicket of
dwarfed and wind-warped cedars and junipers, and once
stopped I was caught, trapped in color and dazzled by the
clarity of the light. Against the descending sun the
battlements were dark and clean-lined, while to the east,
where the uninhibited light poured slantwise, the strange
landscape shouted with color. And the night, far from

being frightful, was lovely beyond thought, for the
stars were close, and although there was no moon
the starlight made a silver glow in the sky. The
air cut the nostrils with dry frost. And for pure
pleasure I collected a pile of dry dead cedar branches
and built a small fire just to smell the perfume of
the burning wood and hear the excited crackle of the
branches. My fire made a dome of yellow light over me,
and nearby I heard a screech owl hunting and a barking
of coyotes, . . . the short chuckling bark of the dark
of the moon. This is one of the few places I have seen
where the night was friendlier than the day. And I can
easily see how people are driven back to the Bad Lands.[2]

The Badlands of the Little Missouri River possessed curious

fantastic beauty and savage desolation in Roosevelt's eyes when

he saw them in 1884. Steinbeck was filled with foreboding at the

dry, sharp, desolate and dangerous unearthly landscape as he

entered the badlands in 1960 or 1961. But both acknowledged that

the Badlands drew one back. This then is the setting of our

furnishing study.

---

2. John Steinbeck, *Travels with Charley* (New York, 1962),
pp. 154-57. In 1960-61 Steinbeck and his poodle, Charley, traveled
across the U. S. from east to west and back. His experiences were
put into this delightful book.

ACKNOWLEDGEMENTS

Several individuals and institutions provided help and advice during the research on this subject. The staff of the State Historical Society of North Dakota searched their collections for material on ranch houses and their furnishings. The staff at Theodore Roosevelt National Memorial Park extended their personal hospitality to me, and Park Interpreter Al Schulmeyer introduced me to Dr. Ralph Hubbard, whose fund of knowledge about early ranching in the northwest is truly amazing. Several members of the Division of History also provided invaluable aid. Francis Wilshin, another Roosevelt admirer, suggested several sources of possible information. The material in Appendix I is the direct result of a suggestion by John D. McDermott, for which I sincerely thank him. Frank Sarles read this manuscript in both draft and final form for errors in punctuation and grammar. Finally, Mrs. Maxine Gresham turned the rough draft into the product you hold in your hand. To all the above people, my thanks and appreciation.

TABLE OF CONTENTS

LIST OF ILLUSTRATIONS

CHAPTER I

Theodore Roosevelt, A Buffalo Hunt and Badlands Ranches

It was a cool September 7 as the Northern Pacific passenger train rumbled across the 300 foot bridge over the Little Missouri and stopped at the town of the same name. A slim young man descended from a coach. As the train pulled away he began to make his way toward a large building looming to the northeast. Upon arrival he hammered on the door and after some time was admitted by the proprietor of the hotel. Muttering curses, the hotel keeper led him upstairs to a large room where fourteen beds were scattered about. Selecting an empty one, the traveler deposited his bags and rifles and went to bed. In the morning he found himself the center of attention. What the others covertly observed was a young slender dude of medium height, with a moustache and glasses, the last being a certain sign of defective moral character.

What they said has been lost to history. Certainly none of them recognized him as member of the New York Assembly, destined to be President of the United States in less than twenty years. Theodore Roosevelt's written comments on his first morning in the Badlands are very slim. He had come to hunt and after breakfast set out to find a guide.

The town of Little Missouri contained only a few buildings. Besides the Pyramid Park Hotel there were several homes, a saloon, a boarding house, and one-quarter mile to the west, a group of log buildings that had housed the company of soldiers detailed to guard the construction crews of the Northern Pacific Railroad from Indian attack. Now it was headquarters for a collection of guides and professional hunters who for a good price would take eastern sportsmen like Roosevelt on hunting trips into the surrounding badlands. It was toward the cantonment that the 24-year-old New Yorker directed his steps.

Roosevelt had come to the Badlands to hunt buffalo and by afternoon he had secured the services of Joseph Ferris, a Canadian about the same age as himself, as guide. Ferris suggested that the most likely place to find buffalo was fifty miles south of the town. He and the manager of the Cantonment, Frank Moore, decided that the best base for the proposed hunt would be Gregor Lang's ranch on the Little Cannonball, 45 miles up the Little Missouri. Ferris suggested to Roosevelt that if they left that afternoon they could spend the night at the ranch of his brother, Sylvane, and William Merrifield, his partner. Another hard day's ride would bring them to the Lang Ranch. Roosevelt agreed, and after tending to several necessary chores in the town they started south to the Chimney Butte ranch of Ferris and Merrifield.

After spending the night there, the two continued their journey south. Roosevelt was now mounted on a horse which he had purchased from the operators of the ranch. Joe Ferris drove the buckboard with their supplies and bedding. On the evening of September 8 they arrived at Lang's small ranch cabin. Though he had ridden nearly forty miles, Roosevelt stayed up until midnight talking to Gregor Lang, the Scottish proprietor. It was raining the next morning and both Ferris and Gregor Lang advised postponement of the first day of the hunt, but Roosevelt had come to hunt buffalo and a little rain would not deter him. With a mental or physical shrug Joe Ferris saddled the horses and they were off at 6 o'clock. In the evening they returned covered with mud, having seen nothing but a few deer. Ferris fell asleep soon after supper, but Roosevelt and Lang sat up until after midnight discussing cattle and politics. The memory of the two sitting at the table, illuminated by a kerosene lamp, was etched into the mind of Lang's 16-year-old son Lincoln. The next morning it was still raining. Ferris suggested waiting, again Roosevelt advocated going out, and again they returned covered with mud. After supper Roosevelt and Gregor Lang picked up their conversation and it was after midnight before they set it aside. This routine went on for three more days. On the sixth morning the sky was clear and the rain had stopped.

By then Roosevelt had nearly succumbed to the lure of becoming a rancher in the valley of the Little Missouri River. But he still wanted to shoot a buffalo. While slipping, sliding, and slogging in the gumbo mud and rain they had seen fresh tracks, but had not secured a shot. With the skies clear Roosevelt and Ferris continued the chase, and after three days of hard riding and camping out on the prairie, plus several missed shots, Roosevelt got himself a prime specimen of a bison bull.[1] The next morning they skinned the animal and brought the hide and head back to the Lang Ranch. Having shot his buffalo Theodore Roosevelt returned to Little Missouri to await word from Sylvane Ferris and William Merrifield, the managers of his newly acquired ranch.

In the midst of the second week of pursuing buffalo, Roosevelt had made up his mind to invest in a Badlands ranch. He first asked Gregor Lang to manage it, but Lang declined because he was involved with other people. Lang suggested Ferris and Merrifield as an alternative. Roosevelt agreed and the men were summoned. Two days later they arrived. That evening and the next day were spent in drawing up an agreement between Roosevelt

1. While Roosevelt was doggedly pursuing a buffalo, the only sizable buffalo herd left in the world was being slaughtered by the Sioux Indians from Standing Rock Agency on their fall hunt. At the beginning of 1883 there were about 10,000 buffalo south of Dickenson, North Dakota, near the headwaters of the Moreau and Grand Rivers. Most of these were killed by professional hide hunters during the spring and summer. The Sioux killed all but about 200 in September and October. In April 1883, when the Langs came to Little Missouri, buffalo shot from passing trains were left to rot. Chester Brooks and Ray Mattison, *Theodore Roosevelt and the Dakota Badlands* (Washington, 1958), p. 19; Lincoln Lang, *Ranching With Roosevelt*, (Philadelphia, 1926), p. 26.

and his two foremen. Roosevelt drew up a check for $14,000
to purchase the cattle the two were running on shares for
Wadsworth and Hawley and to buy a few hundred additional head
in St. Paul. The agreement between the three provided that
Roosevelt was to stock the Chimney Butte or Maltese Cross Ranch
with 400 head of cattle. At the end of seven years the
managers were to return to Roosevelt his original investment
plus half the increase. Any additional cattle bought by Roosevelt
would be managed on the same terms.

By September 23 or 24 Roosevelt was back at the Pyramid Park
Hotel in Little Missouri. Within a day or two he left for
St. Paul and New York, presumably with his hard-won robe and
buffalo head. He was now the owner of a ranch on the Little
Missouri and as such was a part of a society that was still in
a raw frontier state.[2]

Three years before, in September 1880, the Northern Pacific
Railroad had reached the Little Missouri River. The arrival of
the railroad brought eastern sportsmen and professional hunters
to rich game lands of western North Dakota and eastern Montana.

---

2. This report will not deal with all facets of the story
of life along the Little Missouri River, but rather will stick to
a discussion of ranch houses in the western Dakotas and eastern
Montana. For a detailed description of the frontier environment
along the Little Missouri River the following books are excellent:
Brooks and Mattison, *Theodore Roosevelt and the Dakota Badlands;*
Herman Hagedorn, *Roosevelt in the Badlands* (New York, 1921);
Lincoln Lang, *Ranching with Roosevelt;* and Carleton Putnam,
Theodore Roosevelt: The Formative Years, 1858-1886 (New York, 1958).
These four sources were used in the discussion of Roosevelt's
introduction to the Badlands, his buffalo hunt, and the decision
to buy a ranch.

Large-scale buffalo hunting started along the Little Missouri
in the fall of 1881. The same year ranching in the Badlands
began with the establishment of the Custer Trail Ranch five
miles south of Medora by Howard Eaton, a Pennsylvania sportsman,
and hunting guides Frank Moore and Gerry Paddock.[3] Also in 1881
Hiram B. Wadsworth and W. C. Hawley from Minnesota shipped 200
head of cattle to Little Missouri and located the Maltese Cross
Ranch near Chimney Butte. They hired Sylvane Ferris and
A. W. Merrifield to manage it. By the end of 1882, A. C. Huidekoper
of Pittsburg, the Rumsey Brothers of Buffalo, and one or two
others had begun operations. In 1883 the region began to fill
up rapidly as Pierre Wibaux, the Berry-Boice Cattle Company (The
Three Sevens), Tower and Gudgell (OX Ranch) and the Marquis de
Mores plus others took up land along the river and streams that
bisected the Badlands.[4]

The houses built by these ranchers were neither large nor
ornate. The few that deviated from the norm included those of
de Mores with his vast monetary resources, Pierre Wibaux supported
by French capital, and to a lesser extent Theodore Roosevelt. The
typical ranch in the Badlands or on the North Plains was sufficient
for the immediate needs of its residents. Generally there were

---

3. Elwyn B. Robinson, *History of North Dakota* (Lincoln, 1966),
pp. 184-88.
4. Harold Briggs, *Frontiers of the Northwest: A History of
the Upper Missouri Valley* (New York, 1940), pp. 220-222.

two stages in the development of the ranch home. The first structure would be small, often only one or two rooms, and used for a year or two. Then a larger home would be built, often about the time the wife or new bride arrived from the East. This second structure would be the permanent ranch headquarters.

When Roosevelt stayed at the Langs' during his hunting trip of September 1883 the house was "a small log shack with a single window-light in one end, and its gumbo clay roof supported by split cottonwood poles, plentifully decorated with antlers and horns of one kind or another, thrown up there out of the way."[5] The floor was sod, there were two beds, a table, one bench, perhaps a chair or two, and a "fairly serviceable cookstove." In the spring of 1884 a "decent house" was built by the Langs as their family was coming out.

The main ranch house of A. C. Huidekoper was built on the side of a hill. The basement built partially into the hill contained the dining room, kitchen, and store room. In the upper or first floor was the main room, three bedrooms, and a bath, and above that a dormer attic which was used for overflow.[6]

---

5. Lang, *Ranching With Roosevelt*, p. 91. This is how the cabin appeared in August 1883 when Gregor and Lincoln Lang took possession.
6. A.C. Huidekoper, "My Experiences and Investment in the Bad Lands of North Dakota and Some of the Men I Met There," Manuscript Collections, State Historical Society of North Dakota, p. 27. Huidekoper built Shackford about 1885.

In 1885 the Lloyd Roberts family, who had lived at Eaton's Custer Trail Ranch for over a year, began a ranch of their own. They built a house of pine logs three miles north of the Maltese Cross where a long green slope met a semi-circle of grey buttes. It ultimately contained six rooms. In the middle were the living room and kitchen, off the living room were two bedrooms, and from the kitchen one went into a spare room and storage room. The roof was made of split rails covered with tar paper and topped with dirt.[7]

In April 1883, Mrs. Walter Alderson came west with her new husband to his ranch at the junction of Lame Deer Creek and the Rosebud River in eastern Montana. Her first home was a dirt-roof cabin with one door, one window, and two rooms. A gray army blanket served as a door between the kitchen and the bedroom/ living room. Alderson and his partner John Zook began construction of a larger cabin immediately. By August it was ready. Built of hewed logs seven inches square and so well fitted that it looked like a frame house, the building had four rooms.[8]

Roosevelt also built a newer and larger house at the Maltese Cross, though he had no arriving wife or family to spur him on.

---

7. Kate Pelissier, "Reminiscences of a Pioneer Mother," *North Dakota History,* Vol. 24 (July 1957), p. 132.

8. Nannie T. Alderson and H. Smith, *A Bride Goes West* (New York, 1942), p. 71.

When he stopped there in early September the ranch house was
a log building with a dirt roof and floor. The single room
was furnished with a table, three or four chairs, a stove, and
three bunks. A chicken coop was jammed against the rear or
west side of the cabin.[9] After he purchased rights to the
Maltese Cross he suggested to Ferris and Merrifield that a
new cabin be built. By June 1884 the old shack had become a
stable. In its place stood a 1 1/2-story log cabin with a
shingle roof and cellar. The building had three rooms: kitchen,
living room, and bedroom-study for Roosevelt. The other men
and guests slept in the loft above. To the east of the house
was a small garden, the circular horse corral, a large cow
corral, and the hayricks and cow sheds.[10]

Roosevelt perhaps has left the best single description of
a ranch in the Badlands along the Little Missouri or on the
northern plains:

> In the Northern country the ranches vary greatly
> in size: on some there may be but a few hundred head, on
> others ten times as many thousand. The land is still in
> great part unsurveyed, and is hardly anywhere fenced in,
> the cattle roaming over it at will. The small ranches
> are often quite close to one another, say within a couple
> of miles; but the home ranch of a big outfit will not
> have another building within ten or twenty miles of it,
> or, indeed, if the country is dry, not within fifty. The
> ranch house may be only a mud dugout, or a 'shack' made of

9. Theodore Roosevelt, *Autobiography* (New York, 1919), p. 105.
10. Hagedorn, *Roosevelt in the Badlands*, p. 91.

logs stuck upright in the ground; more often it is a
fair sized well made building of hewn logs, divided
into several rooms. Around it are grouped the other
buildings--log stables, cow sheds, and hay ricks, an
outhouse in which to store things, and, on large ranches,
another house in which the cowboys sleep. The strongly
made circular horse corral, with a snubbing post in
the middle, stands close by; the larger cow corral, in
which the stock is branded, may be some distance off.
A small patch of ground is usually enclosed as a vegetable
garden, and a very large one, with water in it. as a
pasture to be used only in special cases.[11]

11. Theodore Roosevelt, *Hunting Trips of a Ranchman* in Works of
Works of Theodore Roosevelt (20 vols. Hermann Hagedorn, editor)
Volume 1 (New York, 1926), pp. 5-6.

CHAPTER II

Kitchen-Dining Room Furnishings

The furnishings found within ranch houses on the Northern

Plains between 1880 and 1900 were determined by several factors.

One of the most important was the financial condition of the

residents. If they were just beginning their ranching operations

the cabin and the furniture would often be sparse and utilitarian.

When they had gained some reward for their efforts and had perhaps

built a new and larger home, the house would contain some

luxuries, and even a surplus of certain materials. Another major

factor was the presence of a woman on the ranch. Often the wife

or bride only came west after the initial work had been done the

first year. A house with only male residents seldom contained

many decorative touches. A woman's presence in the house would

assure that, even if funds were scarce, there would be an attempt

at creating attractive surroundings within the house. Accessibility

to a railroad also was an important factor in determing how well a

home was furnished, for the railroad would bring larger quantities

of consumer goods within reach of those living on ranches. Finally

the personality of the residents would be reflected in the style,

type, and extent of furnishings. The study of ranch house

furnishings which follows will be divided into four sections: kitchen-dining room, living room or parlor, bedrooms, and general or miscellaneous furnishings.[1]

In many of the ranches along the Little Missouri in North Dakota and Montana the kitchen was a large room and served also as the dining area. For this reason these two rooms have been combined in the report. Dominating such a room would be the cook stove. Because of the availability of lignite, a soft impure coal, in the badlands, most of the stoves sold by merchants in Dickenson or Medora, North Dakota, during the 1880s were designed to burn either wood or coal. From illustrations in the Dickenson *Press* in 1883-84 it would appear that the stoves were not excessively large, having a firebox approximately 6 or 8 inches wide and 18 inches long.[2] During the 1880s the following brand names were mentioned by North Dakota newspapers: Garland Stoves, manufactured by the Michigan Stove Company, Jewel Stoves, Universal Oak, and Superior Wood Range.[3] Other stoves common in houses of the area were Charter Oak, Huette and Sons "Riverside," and the Toedt Brothers "Gold Medal."[4] The stoves manufactured or

1. Within the rooms, items will be discussed individually. The decision of where to discuss certain objects was made arbitrarily by the author.

2. See Illustrations.

3. A rapid scanning of the Dickenson *Press* and Bismark *Weekly Tribune* during the years 1883-1890 showed these to be the brands mentioned in advertisements.

4. Sally Johnson, "Maltese Cross Cabin: Reconstruction and Furnishing Plan," MS, 1960. In files of the Museum Branch, National Park Service, Washington.

sold by Montgomery Ward Company would have also been found in the ranch homes of the Northern Plains.

The cost of a stove during the era would have ranged from ten to forty dollars, depending on size and style. In 1877 Daniel W. Longfellow, Post Trader on the Fort Berthold Reservation in North Dakota, listed two stoves at $15 each as part of his inventory.[5] On December 1, 1883, Dickenson Hardware on Villard Street was offering number 8 cookstoves at prices from $10 to $40.[6] The Walter Aldersons, living on Lame Deer in Custer County, Montana, were burned out by Cheyenne Indians on March 18, 1884. Among their losses was "1 cooking stove and fixtures - $50."[7] In 1891 John B. Stoddard, ranching south of Sentinel Butte on the western edge of the State, purchased a stove for $10 from a general merchandise compamy in Mingusville.[8]

5. Daniel W. Longfellow Papers, Manuscript Collections, State Historical Society of North Dakota.

6. Dickenson *Press*, December 1, 1883.

7. Report on losses of Zook and Alderson (Case #4688, Zook and Alderson vs the United States and the Cheyenne Indians), U.S. Court of Claims: Indian Depredations, National Archives, RG 123. Hereinafter cited as Zook and Alderson, Case 4688, U.S. Court of Claims: Indian Depredations, NA, RG 123.

8. John B. Stoddard Papers, Manuscript Collections, State Historical Society of North Dakota. Cited hereafter as SHSND.

Cooking Utensils

It is not possible to present a list of kinds or types of pots and pans used by residents along the Little Missouri during the last twenty years of the last century. Among items mentioned in various narratives are tin bread pans and pie plates; cast iron skillets, frying pans, and tea kettles; a huge iron sugar kettle (used by Mrs. Gregor Lang to prepare a stew for some Indians);[9] a Dutch oven; and some kettles of either cast iron or tin. In determining the exact type of utensils to be used in a refurnished ranch house, considerable reliance could be placed on the catalogue of Montgomery Ward and Company, "The Original Wholesale Grange Supply House," as many homes used the company's mail order services. One advertisement in the Dickenson *Press* for December 22, 1883, described "Something New. A perforated bottom pie plate; no greasing required. Bottom crust will bake as dry and crisp as the top. No more heavy or soggy crusts when baked on this plate. Buy one and try it. For Sale by the Dickenson Hardware Company, Villard St. Dickenson." But, except for this, few specifics were given on pots and pans.

In addition to cooking utensils, other small items found in the kitchen would include a coffee mill similar to the one used

9. Lang, *Ranching with Roosevelt*, p. 210.

by Mrs. Pelissier as a young child at the Custer Trail Ranch
in 1882-83.[10] There would be at least one tin or wood bucket
and a dipper. Dish pans or some other means of washing after
the meal would be present. Churns were more common than
expected in a land with many cattle but few milk cows.[11] Wash-
tubs and boilers, large deep kettles, were also commonly found
in the kitchen or hung outside the door on the side of the
house. Hanging from a nail would be a dish towel.[12]

Cupboards, Shelves, Work Tables, and Washstands

Near the stove were either several shelves or a cupboard
to hold utensils and condiments. Often these were homemade
affairs as simple as a board laid across two pegs driven into
the log wall or a packing case nailed to the wall. In Mrs. Alderson's
first home the cabinet was an old chuck box. In the new house
there was a built-in cupboard with drawers and flour and sugar bins
underneath.[13] Somewhere near the stove and the shelves or cupboards there was a work table used for rolling out pie crusts, and
preparing biscuits and other food. The table would be covered with

---

10. Pelissier, "Reminiscences of a Pioneer Mother," p. 134.
Kate Roberts Pelissier was the daughter of Mrs. Lloyd Roberts, an
early resident along the Little Missouri River.
    11. Ibid.

12. In November 1891, John B. Stoddard bought a dozen dish
towels from Montgomery Ward for 89 cents. Stoddard Papers,
Manuscript Collections, SHSND.

13. Alderson, *A Bride Goes West*, p. 72.

oilcloth to facilitate cleaning. In many cases the table was
homemade and if the kitchen was also used as an eating area
would serve a dual purpose.

In some homes there was a more ornate dining table against
one of the other walls. Finally, a washstand was located outside
the kitchen door or, during the winter, inside the kitchen.
Usually it was a low bench with a basin and a saucer holding a
piece of soap; a towel or old flour sack would hang from a nail
above the bench. There also might be a bucket of water and a
dipper covered with a towel or flour sack. [14] Here the hired hands
or casual visitors would wash up and get a drink of water.

Food and Canned Goods

"Everyone in the country lived out of cans, and you would
see a great heap of them outside of every little shack." [15] The
shelves and cupboards of a ranch home contained a wide variety
of canned goods. The more common ones were corn, tomatoes, canned
milk, and green beans. On March 25, 1877, the inventory of the
Fort Berthold trading post listed the following canned goods:
succotash, black berries, oysters (9 cases) strawberries, and
string beans. [16]   In 1891 Rancher John B. Stoddard purchased

14. Johnson, "Maltese Cross Cabin," p. 20.
15. Alderson, *A Bride Goes West*, p. 40.
16. D. W. Longfellow Papers, Manuscript Collections, SHSND.

large quantities of lima beans, squash, succotash, plum pudding, two gallons of Maple-Honey Syrup, and one case Regi-Swiss milk.[17] In addition to canned goods, the ranchers on the North Plains during the 1880s and 1890s purchased sugar, tea, coffee (often the famous Arbuckle brand),[18] beans, baking powder, flour, and dried fruits in case or 100-pound lots during their yearly or semi-yearly trips to town. Meat was often wild game such as venison, elk, antelope, grouse, or quail. Often this meat was smoked or jerked to preserve it for use later on. Roosevelt, writing to Henry Cabot Lodge in the summer of 1886, noted that "My ranch house looks like an Indian camp now as the other day, when we were out of fresh meat, I shot two elk and some antelope, and the flesh is drying in strips all about."[19] If there was a woman in the house the cupboards might also hold mason jars, sealed with wax or paraffin, containing jams and jellies made from buffalo berries, wild plums, or other fruit.[20]

----

17. John B. Stoddard Papers, Manuscript *Collections*, SHSND.

18. Snowflake and Royal Baking Powder were both advertised in the Dickenson *Press* in 1884 and 1886.

19. Letter written June 19, 1886, from Elkhorn Ranch. Henry C. Lodge, *Selections from the Correspondence of Theodore Roosevelt and Henry Cabot Lodge* (2 vols, New York, 1925), Col. 1, p. 43.

20. After the wives of Bill Sewall and Wilmot Dow arrived at the Elkhorn ranch, homemade jam and jelly became a common item. Hagedorn, *Roosevelt in the Badlands*, p. 311.

Dining Room Table and Chairs

If our typical ranch along the Little Missouri possessed dining room table and chairs, chances were pretty good that they would be home made.[21] The chairs might be benches, or even three or four-legged stools. The table would be made from packing boxes with legs of plain lumber. The chairs even more than the table would reflect the artistic skill of the maker. If the furniture was manufactured, it would probably be of a simple and sturdy design. The chairs would be straight chairs and the table of a comparable design.

Silverware, Dishes, and Tablecloths

A definition of "typical" table furnishings for ranch houses along the Little Missouri River and in eastern Montana is hard to make. For poor settlers or those just beginning in the cattle business, these items would be the plainest and simplest available. Others, who came to the region with some capital, or had achieved a measure of success, might have good silver and china set on fine linen.

In many ranch homes the daily service was tin dishes; tin plated knives, forks, and spoons; and tin cups set on an oilcloth-

---

21. Dr. Ralph Hubbard, personal interview with author, Medora, North Dakota, September 26, 1969. Dr. Hubbard was born in 1886 and came west to visit with his uncle on his ranch on the Musselshell River north of Billings in 1902. Hubbard took a homestead in Montana in 1907 and held it for fifteen years. Between 1922 and 1965, Dr. Hubbard taught at several universities and colleges and worked for the Federal Government. In 1966 he came to Medora and opened a Museum of the Fur Trade and Indian. Dr. Hubbard is an expert taxidermist, has a detailed knowledge of Indian costume and customs, and possesses a remarkable memory.

covered table. In January 1884 the Dickenson Press was
advertising plated knives, forks, spoons, sugar shells, and
butcher knives. Roosevelt ate off of tin dishes while at
the Langs',[22] and V. H. Stickney, a doctor in Dickenson during
the 1880s, and 1890s, recalls the tableware used on round-ups:

> Sitting cross-legged on the ground or reclining
> against a bedroll, we drink our coffee from tin cups
> and eat our food from tin plates, with steel knives
> and forks and pewter spoons. How the memory of those
> savory steaks broiled over the glowing coals comes
> back to haunt a flagging appetite; and the fluffy bis-
> cuits too, and the black coffee with a kick in it like
> a glass of wine.[23]

If the dishes were not tin, they were often porcelain with a design
such as flowers.[24] The table itself would be covered with either
a plain or figured oilcloth.

In contrast to tin tableware and oilcloth is the "snowy
tablecloth and bright silver" used by Isabelle Randall on her ranch
eighteen miles from Bozeman.[25] Nannie Alderson, as so often before,
provides one of the best descriptions of table settings in a more

---

22. Lang, *Ranching With Roosevelt,* p. 103. In 1893, W. H.
Hamilton and his new bride spent the night at the Zoelker Brothers ranch
in northwestern South Dakota and ate off of tin plates. W.H. Hamilton,
"Dakota: An Autobiography of a Cowman," *South Dakota Historical
Collections,* Vol. 19 (1938), p. 573.

23. V.H. Stickney "The Roundup," *North Dakota Historical Quarterly,*
Vol. 1 (October 1916), p. 3.

24. In the archeological work at Roosevelt's Elkhorn Ranch nearly
seventy shards of white porcelain were discovered, much of it having
a blue flower design. Dee C. Taylor, "Archeological Investigations of
the Elkhorn Ranch Site," 1962. Manuscript in files of the Division
of History, OAHP, National Park Service.

25. Isabelle Randall, *A Lady's Ranche Life in Montana* (London, 1887),
p. 110. Mrs. Randall, an English gentlewoman, came west after 1883 and
apparently returned to England within a few years. Her observations on
life in Montana are most amusing.

prosperous ranch house. The second day she was in her new home
on Lame Deer Creek near the Rosebud, her husband built her
a table and benches. On the white oilcloth-covered table,
Mrs. Alderson placed "bright red doilies, my grandmother's silver,
an old fashioned lazy susan in the center with vinegar, salt,
pepper, and mustard bottles; and two delicate china cups and
saucers to raise the tone."[26] Eight months later in December 1883
the Aldersons celebrated their first Christmas in Montana. In the
center of the table was a bowl filled with pine cones and wild
rose berries. On either side were the silver candlesticks sitting
on white doilies with a border of red-edged wheels, and all the
silver she owned. "The doilies did look pretty on the polished
walnut table. I was really proud of myself as I took my seat
at the head of the table, with the baking dish of scalloped oysters
in front of me and the pretty berry spoon to serve them with."[27]
Walter Alderson sat on a churn turned upside down and covered with
a rug. Nannie sat on a dry goods box "made the right height with
my father's copy of Shakespeare and William Cullen Bryant's *Gems of
Prose and Poetry*."

---

26. Alderson, *A Bride Goes West*, p. 30.

27. Ibid, pp. 89-90. For a list of the silver that the Aldersons
had see the itemized list submitted as part of their Indian depredation
claim filed against the Cheyennes and the United States, included
as Appendix I of this report.

The contrast between the simple table settings of ranches like the Langs or others and Aldersons points out the difficulty of determining what is "typical." It is the author's opinion that, in most ranch houses of the Northern Plains, tin or porcelain plates and steel knives, spoons and forks were more common than silver candlesticks and solid silver spoons.

CHAPTER III

Furnishings in the Main Room, Parlor, or Living Room

Every ranch home had a room where the residents spent what leisure hours they had. Whether it was called the main room, parlor, sitting room, or living room, it served as a central point around which the evening or leisure activities of the rancher, his family, his friends, and his employers revolved. The variety of items found within the room was wide, but at a minimum there would be chairs, a small table, lamps, a few books, and some cards or other games to while away the hours.

Chairs

"What true American does not enjoy a rocking-chair?" When he asked this question in *Hunting Trips of a Ranchman*, Theodore Roosevelt declared his own love for a comfortable rocking chair. Photos of the piazza at the Elkhorn show two rockers sitting there. Roosevelt was not alone in his liking for a comfortable rocker. When visiting at the Langs' ranch south of Medora he would rock vigorously as he and Gregor Lang debated the topic of the evening. Often the force of the rocking would cause the chair to move across the floor until it bumped into something and then Roosevelt would straighten it out and resume rocking

and talking.[1] The general style of rocking chair can be seen
from the photo taken of the Elkhorn piazza. They might be made
of golden oak with a flower design,[2] or handmade by an enter-
prising settler to satisfy his wife.[3] Among other items lost
by the Aldersons was a rocking chair valued at ten dollars.[4]

Besides rocking chairs, the sitting room or parlor of a
ranch house would contain plain wooden chairs, benches or stools,
stuffed chairs, and sofas or lounges. The wooden chairs would
be the "loop back cottage type Windsor, of the kind made by the
J. W. Mason Furniture Company and popular from 1860-1890."[5]
In addition to the loop back style there might be some straight
chairs similar to those used in the kitchen. Mrs. Alderson mentions "six small chairs" as part of the living room furnishings
of her new house in August 1883.[6] Often there would be handmade

----

1. Lang, *Ranching With Roosevelt*, p. 217. In 1904 there were
still several rockers in existence that Roosevelt had used. These
were made part of the furnishings of his Maltese Cross Cabin at the
St. Louis Exposition. Interview with Sylvane Ferris and others on
the authenticity of the Maltese Cross Cabin, Dickenson *Press*,
March 19, 1904.

2. Ralph Hubbard of Medora recalled a rocking chair of golden
oak with flowers painted on it at his uncle's ranch on the Musselshell
River in 1902. Mr. Crawford commented that rocking chairs were very
popular and he has two chairs that date from 1888. Ralph Hubbard,
personal interview with author, Medora, North Dakota, September 26, 1969.

3. In the fall of 1878 Mrs. W.M. Lindsay and husband took a homestead in the Red River valley of North Dakota. A year or two later
her husband made a table and rocking chair for her. W.M. Lindsay,
"My Pioneer Years in North Dakota," Manuscript Collections, SHSND.

4. See Appendix I.

5. Johnson, "Maltese Cross Cabin," p. 16. See also photograph
of Huidekoper and others in Illustration section.

6. The house they occupied after the Indians burned their home in
March 1884 was far less luxurious and had a "set of cheap yellow oak
furniture." Alderson, *A Bride Goes West*, p. 114.

chairs, benches, or stools to supplement or replace manufactured chairs. These would be of simple construction. At Roosevelt's Maltese Cross Cabin there were several such benches.[7] Stuffed chairs and sofas or lounges were also found in ranch houses on the Northern Plains during the 1880-1900 period. Generally these were in the homes of settlers who were better off financially.[8] In the mid-1880s both the Aldersons and Randalls had sofas and easy chairs in their Montana ranch houses.[9] By the turn of the century, horsehair sofas and chairs were common. Like so many other items, ranchers often manufactured their own sofas or easy chairs. In 1887 or 1888 the Aldersons improvised a couch out of two Arbuckle coffee cases, some boards and a sougan or comforter.[10] Another ranch had two wooden chairs and a rough bunk covered with blankets which served as a couch during the day and a bed at night.[11] At the turn of the century a bunkhouse near Medora

---

7. Dr. Hubbard in an interview with the author indicated that benches and stools were still common in Montana in 1902.

8. Among the museum items in storage at Theodore Roosevelt National Memorial Park are two stuffed chairs said to have been used by Roosevelt when he stayed at the Ferris Store in Medora. The chairs are in poor condition and have been water damaged, but could be restored to a presentable condition.

9. Mrs. Alderson had an easy chair and a sofa in her home on the Lame Deer, while Mrs. Randall brought a sofa and small arm chair with her from England or the East. Alderson, *A Bride Goes West*, p. 72; Randall, *A Lady's Ranche Life*, p. 11.

10. Alderson, *A Bride Goes West*, p. 166.

11. Describing an American ranch and the house of the "natives," Mrs. Randall viewed with English disdain the squalid conditions under which the people lived. Randall, *A Lady's Ranche Life*, p. 93.

boasted of several easy chairs and a couch that could be made
into a bed.[12]

Carpets and Curtains

A wide variety of floor coverings were used in the ranches in Dakota and Montana. In some the skins of mountain lion, grey wolf, buffalo, coyote or red fox covered the floors.[13] Many of the homes, such as the Roberts' near Medora, had rag carpets. These were made by the lady of the house from strips of rags two or three inches wide braided together. The braids were then sewn together by hand to form round, elliptical or square rugs. Because square rugs tended not to lie flat the first two were the more common shapes.[14] The homes of the wealthier ranchers had commercially produced carpets. Navajo rugs were used in a bunkhouse near the Little Missouri River.[15] Carpet beetles often were a problem, but they could be controlled by spraying a tea of twist tobacco and other herbs on the rugs and carpets.[16]

12. The bunkhouse was on a ranch owned by Sid Monroe. The exact date of the description is not known, but it was probably in the first years of this century. Lewis F. Crawford, *Badlands and Broncho Trails* (Bismark, 1922), pp. 30-31.

13. When Mrs. Alderson arrived at the cabin on Lame Deer Creek near the Rosebud and a hundred miles from Miles City in April 1883 she found the dirt floor of the two-room cabin covered with a white canvas wagon sheet and scattered about were the hides of animals. Alderson, *A Bride Goes West*, p. 29.

14. This description of how a rag carpet was made was given the author by Dr. Ralph Hubbard in an interview at Medora on September 26, 1969.

15. A half-dozen Navajo rugs covered the bunkhouse floor on the Sid Monroe Ranch near Medora. Crawford, *Badlands and Broncho Trails*, p. 31.

16. Ralph Hubbard, personal interview, September 26, 1969.

Curtains were usually made by the lady of the house. The drawing room of Mrs. Randall boasted red curtains, a carpet and writing table and chairs. From the tone of her comments on "ranche life" it is certain that she neither braided a rag carpet nor sewed the curtains. The Lloyd Roberts' ranch boasted inexpensive lace curtains on the windows.[17] In the home burned by Indians, Nannie Alderson had bright curtains and carpet, presumably the former handmade and the latter purchased. After losing all their possessions, the Aldersons moved and resumed ranching on the Rosebud near Muddy Creek. In 1888 Mrs. Alderson made curtains of worn white blankets dyed red with Diamond Dye and trimmed with pieces from a wool lace shawl.[18] The material used for curtains might be either a solid or a print, and often when faded they would be redyed and used until they became so tattered or so dirty that they had to be discarded.

Usually a few pictures and a mirror hung from the walls which were whitewashed, papered, or covered with cretonne, a strong unglazed cotton or linen cloth printed on one or both sides. In some cases walls were plastered, but this was not a common practice. Mrs. Randall mentions pictures and a looking glass hanging on the red wallpaper in the drawing room. In the

17. Pelissier, "Reminiscences of a Pioneer Mother,", p. 132.
18. Alderson, *A Bride Goes West*, p. 174.

Alderson house were two etchings and oval portraits of
Mr. Alderson's parents.[19]

Lamps and Stoves

Light within ranch homes during the 1880s and 1890s was
most often provided by kerosene lamps. Some people used candles[20]
and a few might have had only a dish of tallow and a wick.[21] The
lamps used were of the pressed glass variety in most cases. During
the 1890s the Angle Lamp was popular in the West. Simple in
form, it contained a tank-like fuel reservoir with the wick in
an upward-slanting spout. A clear glass ball globe was attached
to the rim of the wick unit and a milk glass chimney set on top.
Four models were produced. The single-globe lamp would be
attached to the wall, while the two, three, and four-globed style
would be hung from the ceiling.[22] In addition to lamps there would

---

19. During the course of the research on this paper, I found very few references to pictures and mirrors. Dr. Hubbard of Medora commented that mirrors as decorative items were only found in fine homes. It would appear that pictures in the typical badlands ranch were a rare item and should be held to a minimum in any refurnishing. Decorative oval mirrors would be even more rare.

20. Mrs. Pelissier remembers her mother "making little candles out of tallow and a piece of string" and using them to save kerosene. Pelissier, "Reminiscences of a Pioneer Mother," p. 133.

21. In 1878 light in the Lindsay's homestead cabin in the Red River Valley came from "a dish of grease with a rag which I used to sew and read by." Lindsay, "My Pioneer Years," Manuscript Collections, SHSND, p. 4.

22. Lester Beitz, *Treasury of Frontier Relics* (New York, 1966), p. 179. The single-globe model sold for $1.80 during the last decade of the century. A photo of one is included in the illustrations.

be at least one lantern near an outside door for use in
chores in the barn or other locations. Fuel for lamps and
lanterns was inexpensive. In 1877 a gallon of kerosene cost
50 cents at the trading post at Fort Berthold,[23] but eight
years later a case containing ten gallons sold for $2.50 near
Belle Fourche, South Dakota.[24]

Theodore Roosevelt wrote vividly of long winter evenings
sitting around the hearthstone while pine logs roared and
crackled. Fireplaces were found in many of the main rooms of
ranches along the Little Missouri. Pierre Wibaux's "White House"
near Mingusville (Wibaux, Montana) and Huidekoper's home south of
Medora boasted large fireplaces. The Aldersons' stone fireplace
could accommodate a log five feet long. But fireplaces were
not just a right of the rich. Roosevelt describes a night at the
Brophy Ranch on Little Beaver Creek fifty miles from the Elkhorn.
The main house was "a low hut, made partly of turf and partly of
cottonwood logs, and I speedily warmed myself before the fire."[25]
Even with fireplaces in one or two rooms there was still the
necessity of stoves in the other rooms to ward off the below-zero

23. D. W. Longfellow Papers, Manuscript Collections, SHSND.

24. Hamilton, "Dakota: An Autobiography of a Cowman," p. 501.

25. T. Roosevelt, *The Wilderness Hunter* in *Works*, Vol. 2, p. 327.
The visit to the Brophy Ranch occurred in 1884 while Roosevelt was
hunting some lost horses and was caught in a snow storm.

chill of a northern winter. Many of the larger homes were like the seven-room ranch house of Isabelle Randall near Bozeman. The drawing room and den had fireplaces while stoves heated the other rooms.[26] The dining room was heated by an "Angela Stove" which had a transparent front, so that the fire was visible. The door could be opened and "then it is almost as good as an open fireplace."[27] Heating stoves in the Badlands of North Dakota, like cook stoves, were designed to burn either wood or lignite.

Books, Magazines, and Leisure Time Activities

During the leisure hours of summer evenings or the long, cold days of winter, the people on the isolated ranches of the North Plains found time to read and play cards or other games. Because the romance of ranching attracted a wide variety of people, from New York politicians and Pittsburgh capitalists to French noblemen and well-bred Englishmen, the diversity of reading material was considerable. Roosevelt's library, along with Huidekoper's and Wibaux's, was one of the better ones along the Little Missouri. A partial list of authors mentioned in his published writings would include Richard Dodge, John D. Caton, Elliott Coues, Francis Parkman, Washington Irving, Nathaniel Hawthorne, James Fenimore Cooper, James Russell Lowell, Ik Marvel, Matthew

---

26. Randall, *A Lady's Ranche Life*, p. 27.
27. Ibid., pp. 143-44.

Arnold, John Burroughs, Joel Chandler Harris, Sherwood Bonner, George W. Cable, John Keats, Algernon Charles Swinburne, Leo Tolstoy, Edgar Allan Poe, and his friend Henry Cabot Lodge.[28] In addition there would be newspapers and magazines mailed from the east and local newspapers such as *The Bad Lands Cowboy*, published in Medora, and the Dickenson *Press*. Other ranch owners possessed very extensive libraries--Granville Stewart of Montana owned 3,000 volumes and subscribed to all the leading newspapers and magazines.[29] Mrs. Alderson mentions a bookcase and some of her father's books at her home on Lame Deer Creek and note was taken earlier of the use she made of William Cullen Bryant and Shakespeare. Mrs. Randall and her brother-in-law "went in for a course of Shakesphere" one winter, while her husband, Jem, stuck to Tennyson and "such lighter stuff."[30] Not everyone's taste was satisfied by Shakespeare, Parkman, or Coues. Others read *Breeder's Gazette*, and *Heart in Hands*, "in whose columns brunettes and blonds--by their own admission beautiful and highly accomplished were just spoiling to enter connubial bliss."[31]

---

28. Most of these names are contained in *Hunting Trips of a Ranchman, Works*, Vol. 1, p. 11. Roosevelt at the Elkhorn Ranch had "enough books to fill two or three shelves." *Autobiography*, p. 106.

29. Harold Briggs, *Frontiers of the Northwest: A History of the Upper Missouri Valley* (New York, 1940), p. 285.

30. Randall, *A Lady's Ranche Life*, p. 43. Mrs. Randall had been loaned "a whole heap of books" about the same time.

31. Crawford, *Badlands and Broncho Trails*, p. 32. Many a lonesome rancher or cowboy found his connubial bliss through such publications.

There would also be dime novels and other books that were described by one cow puncher, later the Superintendent of Schools in Medora, as trash.[32]

Other means of passing the time included checkers, chess, dominoes, and various card games. Roosevelt on his second night in the Badlands took part in a game of "Old Sledge" at the Maltese Cross Cabin. Some also braided ropes, quirts, and bridles during the long winter months when the land was in the grip of iron cold.[33]

Musical Instruments

Another source of leisure enjoyment was singing and the playing of musical instruments. The usual smaller instruments such as banjos, guitars, violins, and harmonicas were found in fair numbers, but in addition there were pianos and organs in some ranch homes on the Northern Plains.

An integral part of the round-ups along the Little Missouri River in 1884 and 1885 was Howard Eaton's banjo. Around the fire each evening Eaton would play to the delight of the weary men. Besides Eaton's banjo the only other instrument along the Little

---

32. Roosevelt himself was not above reading "trash," this same person sadly informed Herman Hagedorn. *Roosevelt in the Bad Lands*, p. 108.

33. Lang, *Ranching With Roosevelt*, p. 248. Often the quirts were made from old boots. Rawhide for bridles or ropes was out in a circular pattern beginning in the center of the hide. O. Walter Prior, personal interview by Lindon F. Wood, Ranger-Naturalist, Theodore Roosevelt National Memorial Park, Medora, June 26, 1966. Tape on file at the park.

Missouri was the violin which "Fiddling Joe" played at the dances
over Bill Williams' saloon in Medora.[34]   During the winter of
1886-87 the Langs and their hands were able to alleviate the
gloom of the heavy snows and constant blizzards with a piano, a
violin, and guitar plus "our mellifluous voices."[35] On the first
night she spent at the ranch of her husband and John Zook, Nannie
Alderson played her guitar and sang for her husband and the
three other men who worked on the ranch.[36]   Though technically
not a musical instrument the "grind organ" which one of the
hired men at the Roberts' ranch bought for the girls is included
in this section. Along with it came about twenty rollers for
the pieces it would play. To the children "this hand organ was
very wonderful, and we spent many, many, hours playing the records
over and over."[37]   Dave the hired man built a small cabinet with
pigeon holes for each roller. By 1900 or early in the century
there was an accordian, and "an Edison phonograph" with a case
of records in the bunkhouse of the Monroe Ranch.[38]

34. Hagedorn, *Roosevelt in the Bad Lands*, p. 281.
35. Lang, *Ranching With Roosevelt*, p. 247.
36. Alderson, *A Bride Goes West*, p. 31.
37. Pelissier, "Reminiscences of a Pioneer Mother," p. 135.
The grind organ could be played by grinding it with the hand and blow-
ing in an aperture at the same time. The rolls were perforated paper.
Information on the organ was supplied by Edwin C. Bearss, Historian,
Office of Archeology and Historic Preservation, National Park Service.
38. Crawford, *Badlands and Broncho Trails*, P. 31. By 1895 the
phonograph was growing in popularity as means of amustment for the ge
public. Prior to then it had been chiefly a business machine used in
dictation. The Edison Home Phonograph was produced in 1895 in respon
to the wide demand for a cheaper model. Two years later the Edison
Standard appeared at a lower price and in 1899 the Gem, a more modere
priced machine was offered the public. In 1900 the Edison Concert Ph
graph was introduced. It played a record five inches in diameter.
"A Short History of the Phonograph," in *The Phonograph and How to Use
it* (National Phonograph Company, 1900).

In 1884 Gregor and Lincoln Lang completed a larger home in anticipation of the arrival of the family. Among other furnishings was a piano hauled out from town. The first piano the Badlands ever knew, it was the talk of the county. One night 25 cowboys dropped in on the ranch with the request that Lincoln's sister sing for them. In the months that followed such song fests became common, and after the initial shyness wore off several of the visitors joined in, with the resultant concerts being quite lively.[39] About the same time that the Langs were enjoying their concerts, Mrs. Randall was awaiting the arrival of her piano so the drawing room would be complete. It ultimately arrived and by 1885 both the Randalls and another English family living near Bozeman had pianos.[40]

The Lang piano was the first in the Badlands, but a year or two later Roosevelt added an organ to the furnishings of the Elkhorn ranch. He had purchased it for the use of Mrs. Sewall and Mrs. Dow, the wives of his managers at Elkhorn. They used it,

---

39. Lang, *Ranching With Roosevelt*, pp. 162-64. Nathan Ford of St. Paul, Minnesota, was offering bargains on Knabe and Fisher pianos and Clough and Warren organs in the Dickenson *Press* in late 1883 and early 1884.

40. Randall, *A Lady's Ranche Life*, pp. 15, 27, and 131.

among other things, to play hymns.   In March of 1893, W. H.

Hamilton returned to the Dakotas with a new bride. They were

met by his father at Belle Fourche. Because his wife wanted

to take her organ to the ranch in the Cave Hills, they waited

in Belle Fourche until April 15 when it arrived, then loaded

it and a few other housekeeping articles into the wagon and

started for the ranch. They spent a night at the Zoelker

Brothers Ranch. Upon learning that they had an organ, the

men unloaded it and during the evening had a concert with the

organ and fiddle. In the morning it was placed back on the

wagon and continued on to the Cave Hills in northwestern
42
South Dakota.

---

41. On September 12, 1963, the Theodore Roosevelt Association of New York City transferred, as a gift, to Theodore Roosevelt National Memorial Park a Mason and Hamlin organ, described on the Museum Catalogue Card as patented on January 20, 1874. It has a five-octave keyboard with five stops. The mahogany cabinet is in very good shape, but the left front leg of the bench has been broken and repaired. The card notes it is in unusable condition. Museum Folder 93, Theodore Roosevelt National Memorial Park, North Dakota.

In November 1961 Superintendent Wallace McCaw of TRNMP wrote to several people who might have knowledge of the existence of an organ at Roosevelt's Elkhorn Ranch. On December 1, 1961, Herman Hagedorn replied giving the information included in the text. Hagedorn learned this from William W. Sewall, Roosevelt's manager. Ibid.

42. Hamilton, "Dakota: An Autobiography of a Cowman," pp. 570-73. Hamilton had come to the Dakotas in 1885.

Besides those items already mentioned, there would be a variety of other things in the main room of the house. The mantel over the fireplace or shelves within the room would contain a variety of diverse items. There might be several pipes, a sack of Bull Durham tobacco, photographs, something as different as boxing gloves, a small vase, a box of rifle or pistol shells, mementoes of a trip to Chicago or St. Paul, or any other items that would give the room an individual character. Within the room there could be a bird cage or some house plants such as were at the Roberts' ranch.[43] A large Bible with colored pictures and a place for family records might be on a stand in a corner or in the bookcase.[44] On one wall there might be a large wall clock.[45] Elk antlers or deer horns over the doors or along the walls would hold rifles and heavy overcoats of wolfskin or coonskin and caps and gauntlets of otter fur or beaver fur.[46] The presence of a lady in the house would be accentuated by some half-finished knitting

---

43. Pelissier, "Reminiscences of a Pioneer Mother," p. 132. The Robertses had a canary bird.

44. Kate Pelissier, "My Mother," in Old Timers File, TRNMP, p. 1. The information in this article supplements that in the article in *North Dakota History*.

45. Ibid. In *Badlands and Broncho Trails*, p. 31, Lewis F. Brawford notes the presence of an eight-day Thomas clock encircled by a pair of elk horns in the Monroe bunkhouse.

46. Roosevelt, *Hunting Trips of a Ranchman*, p. 11.

on the arm of a chair or a shelf.   The presence of animal skins
on the floor as rugs might be complemented by several mounted
heads of elk, bear, antelope, deer, or buffalo. There could be
other objects within the room to add character and individuality
to this, the living room of the main ranch house.

---

47. Mrs. Roberts, after the mysterious disappearance of
Lloyd Roberts in the fall of 1886, knit stockings and mittens
not only for her girls, but also for sale to cowboys of the region.
Pelissier, "Reminiscences of a Pioneer Mother," p. 135.

CHAPTER IV

Bedroom Furnishings

In both the small, two-room cabin and the larger house
completed in August 1883, the Alderson's bedroom also served as
the main room or living area: "Our bedroom with its huge fireplace. . . was again the living room for all when the day's work
was done." This rather unique arrangement was the idea of Walter
Alderson and was enthusiastically supported by his wife: "I
never regretted the arrangement where we shared our home with our
nice cowboys, and with every stray rider who came our way."[1] A
common arrangement by necessity in the small cabins containing one
or two rooms, the arrangement was singular in larger ranch houses.
In these the bedroom was just that -- the room where the bed or
beds were.

Beds and Bedding

In many cases bedsteads in ranches along the Little Missouri
and in Eastern Montana were homemade. Lang provided a description
of such beds -- coverless hay mattresses supported by light cottonwood poles -- in describing the cabin on Little Cannonball Creek
in 1883.[2] Discussing his overnight stay at the Brophy Ranch in

---

1. Alderson, *A Bride Goes West*, pp. 72-73.
2. Lang, *Ranching with Roosevelt*, p. 91.

1884, Roosevelt mentions two bunks, one above the other: "I
climbed into the upper, leaving my friends, who occupied the
lower sitting together on a bench recounting different
incidents in the careers of themselves."[3]   The usual bed
was constructed of posts or 4x4 lumber with slats running length-
wise for springs. Over this a blue and white striped mattress
ticking stuffed with hay, grass, or, less likely, corn husks,
was placed. Cowboys usually had double blankets on the beds
but sheets were a luxury. Hide robes were sometimes used instead
of blankets for covering.[4]   While the Aldersons had a manufactured
bedroom suite in their home on Lame Deer Creek, they later used
homemade beds on the ranch they occupied in 1888. Mrs. Alderson
in an attempt to beautify their home, made counterpanes of red
calico to hide the rough, ugly legs of the beds.[5]

When manufactured furniture was utilized it might be as
fancy as the walnut bedroom set that had been shipped all the way
from St. Joseph, Missouri, as a wedding gift to the Aldersons

---

3. Roosevelt, *The Wilderness Hunter* in *Works*, Vol. 2, p. 327.
Sally Johnson in her furnishing plan for the Maltese Cross cabin
notes that Mr. Chris Rasmussen in an interview with her on July 29,
1959, stated that decked bunk beds were not used in the Dakotas.
From Roosevelt's comments, in at least one cabin at one time they
were. Furnishing Plan, p. 16.
4. Interview with Chris Rasmussen by Sally Johnson on July 29,
1959, in Johnson "Furnishing Plan Maltese Cross Cabin," p. 16.
5. Alderson, *A Bride Goes West*, p. 174.

from their partner, Johnny Zook. Roosevelt's furniture was described as "plain dark stained -- cheap."[6] The bunkroom in the third home of the Aldersons, built after the Cheyenne had burned their second house, contained plain iron bedsteads on which the roundup beds of the men were spread.[7] During the early 1890s, folding beds were popular. These folded up to form wardrobes or cabinets with mirrors, shelves for bric-a-brac, and even drawers. The Aldersons had two such beds, one purchased in 1893 and the other won at a raffle somewhat later. The second one was raffled off since no one could afford to buy it in the post-1893 depression. This king of all folding beds even possessed a full length mirror -- "For the first time since I left West Virginia, I was able to see my feet."[8]

Cradles and children's beds, like those for adults, were often homemade. In August 1886 Mrs. William Sewall and Mrs. Wilmot Dow gave birth to boys just one week apart. On August 16, a few days after the arrival of the second child, Bill Sewall began to make a cradle big enough for both babies. Roosevelt upon arrival at the ranch commented that he was making too much noise, and should be more quiet for the babies sake. Sewall told him

---

6. In 1957 several original drawings of the Maltese Cross Cabin were discovered at the State Historical Society of North Dakota. One of them contained a plan showing furnishings and a brief description of the furniture. Cited in Johnson, "Maltese Cross Cabin," figure 7 following page 9.

7. Alderson, *A Bride Goes West*, p. 147.

8. Ibid., pp. 253-56. Folding beds would only be found in the homes of extremely well-to-do ranchers. From the comments of Mrs. Alderson, not even they were buying such items after the depression of 1893.

that the noise was good for them.

Double blankets were the usual bedding in the ranch houses of the plains. Though sheets were not common, Roosevelt noted that he had clean sheets at the Elkhorn ranch in 1886. Buffalo robes were used as bedding also. Roosevelt used a robe sewed up at the sides and end while traveling light and carrying [10] his bed behind his saddle. Hagedorn describes how the fatigued Joe Ferris in September 1883 would wrap himself into his buffalo robe, or roll "nigh dead into his buffalo robe and Roosevelt talked cattle and politics with Gregor Lang until [11] one and two in the morning."

Other Bedroom Furniture

Roosevelt's bedroom furniture has already been described as plain, dark stained and cheap. Besides the bed it included a washstand, bureau, and table. Over the washstand there would be a mirror and below the mirror a shelf holding a razor, shaving mug and brush, and a leather strop. On the washstand would be a pitcher and wash basin of either simple ironstone or perhaps something a bit fancier. There would be a lamp in a bracket nailed to the wall for light in the early dawn or after dusk. A towel would be nearby.

---

9. William W. Sewall, *Bill Sewall's Story of T.R.* (New York, 1919), p. 91.

10. Roosevelt, *Hunting Trips of a Ranchman,* in *Works,* vol. 1, p. 28.

11. Hagedorn, *Roosevelt in the Badlands,* p. 28. Hagedorn may or may not be indulging in vivid description in this discussion of events at Langs.

In the fall of 1883 the Aldersons were enjoying the luxuries of their new home. The bedroom furniture was walnut and the dresser and wash stand had marble tops. There was a carpet and curtains as well.[12] On the washstand was a pitcher and basin of cream-colored china with flowers painted on it. The edges were gilt. It, like the bedroom furniture, had come from the East.[13] All this was destroyed in the fire of March 1884 or by the Cheyennes. Four years later they were living on the Rosebud River and Muddy Creek. One of their cowboys built Mrs. Alderson a rough bureau. It had no drawers, but rather shelves which she covered with cretonne.[14] Mrs. Alderson also purchased a carpet for the bedroom with profits from the sale of a steer she had raised from a calf. Other bedroom sets would be plain or fancy, depending on the financial condition of the owners and other factors. Most would conform to the description of Roosevelt's room with the possible addition of carpeting. The three examples given above would span from poor to middle to upper class.

_____

12. Alderson, *A Bride Goes West,* p. 72.

13. Ibid., p. 104. There was no doubt a third item in the set - that necessary utensil which slips beneath the bed.

14. Ibid., p. 166.

In addition to the usual bedroom sets, other items that might be in the bedroom would be a sewing machine,[15] trunks for the storage of clothes,[16] and clothes themselves. The working clothes of the rancher or his wife were often hung on a nail or peg driven into the wall.[17] From these pegs would hang the items that were the tools of the ranchor's trade as well as the identifying symbols of the cowman. Pants were made of dark wool with a pattern of stripes or small checks and were close fitting with slash or western style pockets. It was the 1890s before blue denim "Levis" began to gain popularity. Shirts were often homemade of a pullover style with buttons halfway down the front, and also were dark color with or without a design. Most

---

15. Mrs. Pelissier spoke of "that much prized sewing machine" in the Roberts' ranch house. Mrs. Lindsay in northeastern North Dakota 35 miles from Grand Forks had a sewing machine in 1878. Pelissier, "Reminiscences of a Pioneer Mother," p. 135; Lindsay, "My Pioneer Years," Manuscript Collections, SHSND.

16. Chests or trunks, often covered with leather, were used to store clothes or other items. Sweet grass was often used to keep bugs out of such trunks or chests. Ralph Hubbard, personal interview with author, Medora, North Dakota, September 26, 1969. Mr. Hubbard has several such trunks in his collection.

17. Alderson, *A Bride Goes West*, p. 43. Johnson, "Maltese Cross Cabin Furnishing Plan," p. 17. The discussion that follows will be devoted chiefly to men's clothing. Women wore cotton or wool dresses of rather plain or simple design for daily work. Mrs. Lloyd Roberts possessed two good dresses, doubtless packed away for special occasions. One was a wine-colored cashmere trimmed with flat, dollar-sized buttons. With it she wore white linen cuffs with real gold cuff links and long pendant earrings of Black Hills gold. The other was a riding habit of green lady's cloth. It was double breasted with cut-steel buttons the size of a quarter. The swallow-tail back was trimmed with the same buttons. With this she wore stiff white linen cuffs and collar and a black derby. Pelissier, "Reminiscences of a Pioneer Mother," p. 132.

shirts were heavy and made of wool or flannel, since jackets were not used. Silk shirts, though expensive, were popular since they turned the wind. Nearly everyone wore a vest and used the four extra pockets it provided to keep small items such as cigarette makings. Jackets or outer coats were often the "sourdough" type made of heavy material and lined with blanketing or flannel. Everyone carried a slicker -- generally yellow, made of canvas or duck, and waterproofed with linseed oil. Socks were wool and often homemade. Boots reached nearly to the knee, had a two-inch heel and were most often made of black calf leather. Ready-made boots cost $7 and special order boots cost twice as much. Chaps were not worn along the Little Missouri in the early 1880s. After the Texans reached there in large numbers, their use increased. Most were the closed leg or shotgun style; later on the open or batwing chaps became more common. Gloves were used by most cowmen to protect their hands while roping or doing other work. These gloves were often made by Busby of California. Bandanas of bright, cheap cotton were tied loosely about the neck. The hat and crowning glory of the cowman was often Stetson's "Boss of the Plains" with a 3 1/2-inch brim and 7-inch crown. The crowns were undented

or dented depending on where the man was from -- Texas or some-[18]
place else.

Roosevelt, who delighted in dressing like the boys,
described his outfit as follows: "I wear a sombrero, silk
neckerchief, fringed buckskin shirt, sealskin chaparajos or
riding trowsers (sic); alligator hide boots; and with my pearl
hilted revolver and beautifully finished Winchester rifle,
I feel able to face anything."[19]

---

18. Most of the information on dress and equipment was
taken from Don Rickey's excellent report on the subject. For
further details the reader is referred to it. Rickey, "Cowboy
Dress, Arms, Tools, and Equipment as Used in the Little Missouri
Range Country and the Medora Area in the 1880s," 1957, Manuscript
in the files of the Division of History, OAHP, National Park
Service.

19. Letter dated Chimney Butte Ranch, August 17, 1884. Anna
Roosevelt Cowles, *Letters from Theodore Roosevelt to Anna Roosevelt
Cowles, 1870-1918* (New York, 1924), p. 62.

CHAPTER V

And Other Ranch House Furnishings

Rifles and Revolvers

Roosevelt's mention of his revolver and rifle indicated
the role these weapons played in the daily life of cowmen.
Though not as prevalent as modern Hollywood or television
westerns depict, rifles and pistols were common along the
Little Missouri frontier. Much of the fresh meat available
was wild game killed by the rancher or his men. And in some
situations the handgun made the difference between life and
death.

With the end of Indian hostilities the carrying of rifles
and carbines by cowboys decreased. It became a weapon to be
used while on specific business such as hunting or riding line.
Many cowboys would supplement their income during the winter
as market hunters shooting game for sale to the railroad or
local hotels. Though there might be a few Sharps rifles carried
by cowmen, the most popular weapon was the Winchester carbine or
rifle and usually it was the 1873 model in 44/40 calibre. Other
long guns were carried by cowboys besides Winchester carbines
and Sharps rifles. These included the "rolling block" Remington,
a strong single-shot breech-loading rifle introduced toward the

end of the Civil War, and a lever-action Colt carbine similar to the Winchester.[1]

Roosevelt, like other gentlemen ranchers, had a variety of rifles and carbines at his disposal. In September 1883 he had a heavy Sharps rifle that fired a 1 1/4-ounce slug, a .50 calibre double-barrelled English express, and a Winchester Model 1876 that was a .45/70 calibre and designed for large game, such as buffalo. He soon abandoned the first two because they were not repeaters and had a hard recoil. In their place he acquired a .40/90 Sharps for long range work, a .50/115 six-shot Ballard, plus the .45/70 half-magazine Winchester.[2] Roosevelt later obtained two double barreled shotguns and a double barreled sixteen gauge shotgun with a .40/70 rifle mounted beneath it. The latter he used while riding about near his ranch and thus was ready for both birds and larger game.[3]

Because rifle ammunition was quite expensive during the 1880s, many if not everyone reloaded their empty cartridges. Several firms

1. This brief discussion of long guns used by cowmen in the Western Dakotas is based on Rickey's "Cowboy Dress, Arms, Tools and Equipment," pp. 36-41.

2. Roosevelt in *Hunting Trips of a Ranchman*, pp. 26-27, describes the weapons he had at his disposal. He becomes lyrical in describing the Winchester .45/70, "the best weapon I have ever had, and I now [1885] use it almost exclusively, having killed every kind of game with it from grizzy bear to a bighorn. It is handy to carry . . ., and comes up to the shoulder as readily as a shotgun; it is absolutely sure and there is no recoil to jar and disturb the aim, while it carries accurately quite as far as a man can aim with any degree of certainty; and the bullet, weighing three quarters of an ounce, is plenty large enough for anything on this continent."

3. Ibid., p. 28.

offered reloading equipment and the making of lead bullets

and reloading of shells was another occupation that [4]
filled the long winter evenings or other leisure moments.

While rifles were not owned by everyone and carried con-
tinually by very few, the pistol or revolver was part of
almost every cowpuncher's equipment, and worn by most. It was
a weapon of self-defense, but was also used to hunt game or
kill wolves or coyotes, in signalling, and as a source of
amusement or sport. Nearly everyone who wore a gun carried it
in a large open-top holster hung on a cartridge belt. The
most popular type of revolver in the 1880s was the single
action Colt model 1873. Made originally for the army in
calibre .45 it was available in a variety of other calibres and
barrel sizes including .44, .41, and .44/40 [5] The Army revolver
had a 7 1/2-inch barrel, while most of the pistols used by
cowboys had shorter barrels, from 4-3/4 to 7 inches. Most
cowboy Colts were metallic blue with molded black hard-rubber
grips, though a few had pearl, bone, or ivory grips. Though
Colt dominated, revolvers manufactured by Smith & Wesson and

---

4. Rickey, "Cowboy Dress, Arms, Tools, and Equipment,"
p. 40.

5, The .44/40 ammunition would fit both the pistol and
the Winchester Model 1873 rifle and carbine.

Remington also were used on the Dakota-Montana frontier of the 1880s.[6] Roosevelt noted that every ranchman carried "a long 45 Colt or Smith and Wesson, by preference the former."

Though many cowmen wore their guns to town and others would tuck the revolver in the belly band of the trousers underneath their coat, Roosevelt was dissuaded from this by Arthur Packard, publisher of *The Bad Lands Cowboy*. Packard suggested that Roosevelt leave his weapon in the newspaper office and reinforced the suggestion by asking a local gunman to demonstrate his skill:

> William Roberts was a two-gun man of the type that considered a trigger a useless encumbrance on a revolver. He could jerk a revolver from a holster with his forefinger, twirl it half over, engage the hammer with his thumb and let it fall on the cartridge so quickly that it was impossible to see all the movements. . . . I called to William and asked if he could hit two tomato cans, one with each gun, while the cans were in the air. William said he could and Roosevelt and I rustled up a can each for the trial. Standing in line with William and about ten feet on each side, Roosevelt and I tossed the cans in the air. William had been standing with his hands at his sides, but the first two shots came while the cans were on the way up, then came two more as the cans started to come down and then a fusillade sent the cans rolling after they had struck the ground. Probably not five seconds had passed before ten shots were fired and the cans showed five bullets had passed through each. It was a wonderful exhibition, but I had seen William do it before and it was the deciding reason why I never carried a gun in the Bad Lands.[7]

6. See Rickey, "Cowboy Dress, Arms, Tools and Equipment," pp. 26-35, for an extended discussion of weapons and holsters.

7. Hagedorn, Bad Lands Notes transcript of interview with Arthur Packard as cited in Putnam, *Theodore Roosevelt: The Formative Years*, p. 462.

Theodore took the lesson to heart and did not wear his guns
to town. He later wrote in one of his books that a revolver
was a "mere foolish encumbrance for any but a trained expert
and need never be carried."[8]

Except in one instance there was little mention of toys
for children who lived in ranches along the Little Missouri.
Presumably most toys were homemade with a few purchased from
the always available mail order houses. Theodore Roosevelt
took pity on William Sewall's older girl who had "neither play-
mates or playtoys." He requested his sister Anna purchase the
following toys, charging her to make sure they were sturdy and
cheap: a big colored ball, some picture blocks, some letter
blocks, a little horse and wagon, and a rag doll.[9] A month
later, when the toys had not arrived, Roosevelt wrote to his
sister again asking what had happened to his request for "some
toys (blocks, a ball, a woolly dog, and a rag doll, etc) for
the forlorn little mite of a _____ child."[10] A week later
the toys arrived and he notes that they will be "priceless

---

8. Putnam, *Theodore Roosevelt*, p. 462.

9. Letter to Anna Roosevelt dated Medora, May 15, 1886.
Cowles, *Letters from Theodore Roosevelt to Anna R. Cowles, 1870-
1918*, p. 80.

10. Letter to Anna Roosevelt dated Medora, June 19, 1886.
Ibid., p. 83.

treasures to the poor little Seawall (sic) mite."[11]

In March of 1884 Walt and Nannie Alderson's first child
was born and two days later their house was burned down by the
Cheyennes. Mrs. Alderson remained in Billings while her husband
and Mr. Zook built a new house. By July the baby girl was becoming quite heavy, but, lacking a baby carriage, Mrs. Alderson
continued to carry her in her arms. One evening she was called
into the hotel parlor and discovered her baby in "as nice a baby
carriage as I have ever seen." The local stockmen had got
together and bought it for her. The carriage served for her four
children and was then handed down to a neighbor.[12]   Though baby
carriages may not have been common on the cattle frontier,
Mrs. Lindsay had brought her baby buggy with her to their homestead
in the Red River Valley north of Grand Forks, North Dakota, in
1878.[13]

----

    11. Letter to Anna Roosevelt, Medora, June 28, 1886. Elting E.
Morison, ed., *The Letters of Theodore Roosevelt* (8 vols., Cambridge,
1951), Vol. 1, p. 104. The child was about the same age as his
daughter Alice, born February 1884, but Roosevelt's concern for her
did not stop him from critical comments on her as a table companion.
"I don't appreciate it as a table companion, especially when fed on
or rather feeding itself on, a mixture of syrup and strawberry jam
(giving it the look of a dirty little yellow haired gnome in war-
paint); but I wish the poor forlorn little morsel had some playtoys."
Ibid., Vol. 1, p. 100.

    12. Alderson, *A Bride Goes West*, pp. 113-14.

    13. Lindsay, "My Pioneer Years," Manuscript in Collections,
SHSND.

A Garden and Willow Stake Fencing

Near the ranch home there might be a small garden containing potatoes, peas, lettuce, tomatoes, other vegetable and perhaps watermelons or cantaloupe. There might be a few flowers along the edge.[14] The area would be fenced, very possibly with a willow stake fence. Built of willow saplings the size of a man's thumb, with two or more strands of wire woven through them, and reinforced by posts placed intermittently, it was some protection against rabbits.[15]

Medicines

A reading of advertisements in newspapers of western North Dakota causes one to wonder how the pioneers conquered the land if they needed all the medications offered. In November 1883 the Dickenson *Press* contained advertisements for Allen's Lung Balsam for coughs, colds, and croup; Hostetters Stomach Bitters; Tutts Pills for Torpid Bowels; Mexican Mustang Liniment; and Parsons Purgative Pills. Roosevelt suffered from "cholera morbus" and other ills. The shelves of the Elkhorn Ranch held a certain amount of medicinal preparations for him and others. These included cures for liver ills (Hoods Pills, Lowell, Massachusetts)

---

14. This is a composite description of the gardens at Aldersons and the Roberts' ranch south of Medora. *A Bride Goes West*, p. 53, and Pelissier, "Reminiscences of a Pioneer Mother," p. 133.

15. This type of fencing was described by Dr. Ralph Hubbard in an interview with the author, Medora, September 26, 1969.

and long necked bottle 6 1/4 inches high and 2 inches square from H. J. Frazer, Chemist and Druggist, Ottawa.[16]

Generally found in the kitchen, the food safe or pantry cabinet was a common sight throughout the United States. Models used in the western United States differed in two ways from those in the East. First the frontier model had perforated side panels and cabinet doors. This was intended to facilitate the circulation of air through the cabinet. In the arid regions of the plains and Southwest, proper ventilation was of prime importance in preserving food. The panels were usually of light-gauge tin with holes punched in decorative patterns. Occasionally the panels would be of wood with tiny drilled perforations. Second, the wood used in the western model was pine, oak, ash, or chestnut rather than the more expensive walnut, cherry, or maple used in eastern models. The difference can be attributed to the need of western settlers for a less expensive cabinet. Generally food safes sold for seven or eight dollars on the western frontier.[17]

There were many other items of furniture that might be found in homes on the Dakota-Montana ranch frontier beyond those already discussed in this report. There would be cuspidors or at least

---

16. Taylor, "Archeological Investigations Elkhorn Ranch," pp. 84-94. Taylor found many whole bottles during his work including a shoe polish bottle with stopper and dauber, several wine bottles, and a sarsaparilla bottle (from C.I. Hood, Apothecaries, Lowell, Mass).

17. Beitz, *Treasury of Frontier Relics*, p. 172.

52

a pail half full of ashes, as at the Monroe ranch near Medora.

Wine or liquor bottles would be in evidence in some homes.

The Roberts children had moccasins with elkskin soles and deerskin

uppers. Somewhere there might be a tin bathtub; Roosevelt had a

rubber bathtub at the Elkhorn Ranch.[18] Most of the furnishings

typical of a ranch on the North Plains have been mentioned.

Those that have not are items that would add an individuality

to the rooms and tell something about the men, women, and children

who lived in the ranch houses of the Badlands during the decade

that Theodore Roosevelt called it his home for a part of each

year.[19]

18. Roosevelt, *Autobiography*, p. 106.

19. A study of the illustrations accompanying this report
will add to the reader's understanding of the small additional items
which filled the homes of the ranch owner and his family.

APPENDIX I

On March 18, 1884, a small band of Cheyenne Indians
under the leadership of Black Wolf burned the Alderson
ranch house and destroyed nearly all the furnishings. The
reason for this was the result of one of Alderson's men
attempting to shoot the hat off Black Wolf's head and
grazing his skull. The white culprit escaped from the
country, while several of the Indians were captured and
imprisoned for their actions. In late April both Alderson
and Zook filled claims against the government for Indian
depredations. The listing of their losses provides the
best single description of what an eastern Montana ranch
in 1883-84 contained. The Alderson Ranch was described by
the agent for the Cheyennes, William Dyer, as the "finest
ranch I know of in the country."

The material in Appendix I is from United States Court of
Claims: Indian Depredations, Case #4688 (Zook and
Alderson vs The United States and the Cheyenne Indians),
1884. National Archives, Record Group 123.

No. 3245.

3rd Com. of Indian Affairs
June 20th 1887.

Submits a report upon claim of
Zook & Aldersan, a business firm,
composed of John J. Zook, & Walter W. Aldersan, of Custer County, Montana, for the sum of $6337,
four and one half cents, on account of a depredation alleged
to have been committed by Cheyenne Indians, in Custer County,
Montana, on March 18th, 1884.
Recommends allowance of $3950, 28

Letter to 90 June 1787

Refer in reply to the following:

Depredation.
No. 5345

4 Enclosures.   Packages,

Department of the Interior,

OFFICE OF INDIAN AFFAIRS,

Washington, June 20 Th 1887,

The Honorable

    The Secretary of the Interior

Sir:--

    I have the honor to submit herewith, a report upon the
claim of Zook & Aldersan, a business firm composed of John J.
Zook, and Walter W. Aldersan, of the County of Custer, and the
Territory of Montana, for the sum of $6,337,4 and one half
cents, which was placed upon the files of this office, on the
5th day of May, 1884, and originated, as claimants charge, on account of a depredation, said to have been committed, by Cheyenne Indians, in Custer County, aforesaid, on the 18th day of
March, 1884,

    The claimants each file a separate petition, and in
substance, they are the same, and for the purpose of avoiding
an unnecessary iteration of the same matter, this report will
contain an abstract of the petition of said Walter W. Aldersan's petition, and added thereto, any additional statements,

made by the other member of the firm, John I. Zook.

The petition of said Walter W. Aldersan, was duly executed on the 22nd day of April, 1884, and the petition of John I. Zook, was duly sworn to, on the 26th of April 1884. The substance of each of said petitions, is as follows:—"That the firm of Zook & Aldersan, until the 18th day of March, 1884, had their head quarters on "Lame Deer Creek," about three miles from its mouth, where it emptied into the Rosebud River, in said Custer County, That the improvements belonging to said firm at said point, consisted of one dwelling house, one log store-house, one stable, two corrals, and other improvements, which are more particularly stated, in the schedule, hereto attached.

That on the 18th day of March, 1884, the said improvements and the personal effects, and all of the property mentioned in the said schedule, were by force, and arms, destroyed by a band of Cheyenne Indians, under the leadership of Chief "Black Wolf."——That some of the property taken by said Indians, was afterwards recovered, by said firm, the particulars of which are stated in said schedule, hereto annexed, That the property so destroyed or stolen was situated upon land, settled upon by these claimants, under the laws of the U.S., the same being at the time of the said settlement, vacant Public land,, subject to preemption, by citizens of the U.S., and not being within the limits of any Indian reservation.

That the said dwelling-house, was the residence of claimant, Aldesan, his family, and the employes of said firm, and was constantly properly guarded. That no compensation has ever been made to said firm, for said loss, nor has said firm, ever recovered any of said property, except as hereinafter stated, in said annexed bill of particulars, and that said partners, nor either of them, have in any way sought private satisfaction or revenge. That one Brown Toliafero, whose affidavit is hereto annexed, was present at the time of the commission of the said depredation."

The schedule referred to in the petition, of said claimant of the property lost, its value, together with the property recovered, and the additions made to the same, by one of the claimants, J. I. Zook, is as follows:—

Marble top bed-room set,	$180,00
I Sofa,	20,00
I Easy chair,	20,00
I Rocking chair,	10,00
I Chamber set,	18,00
5 Pictures,	38,00
I Writing desk,	20,00
I Carpet,	25,00
I Mantle Lambrequin,	6,00
I Table cover,	4,00
I Centre table,	3,00
I Bracket,	5,00
3 Char tidies,	5,00
I Sofa pillow,	3,00
I Plush pin cushion,	2,00

I Woven wire spring for bed,————————————————$ 8,00
2 WOOl mattresses,————————————————————— 20,00
I Hair mattress,——————————————————————— I5,00
I Clock,———————————————————————————— 5,00
I Pair vases,——————————————————————— 3,00
3 Lamps,————————————————————————————— 6,00
9 Pair sheets,————————————————————————— 25,00
3 Dozen napkins,——————————————————————— I2,00
3 Table cloths,————————————————————————— 7,50
8 Pair pillow cases,———————————————————————— 5,50
I Pair pillows,————————————————————————— 6,00
2 Pair pillows,————————————————————————— 8,00
IO Pair blankets,——————————————————————— I33,00
2 Comforts,———————————————————————————— 8,00
I Marseilles bed spread,———————————————————— 6,00
I and a half doz. towels,————————————————————— 9,00
3 Curtains,————————————————————————————— 7,50
2 Bed steads,———————————————————————————— I4,00
2 Trunks,——————————————————————————————— 25,00
I Bear robe,———————————————————————————— I5,00
3 Buffalo robes,————————————————————————— 30,00
I Mountain lion robe,————————————————————— IO,00
I Fox mat,——————————————————————————————— 2,50
6 Wolf mats,————————————————————————————— I8,00
4 Beaver skins,————————————————————————— I8,00
I Skunk mat,——————————————————————————— 3,00
I Guitar,———————————————————————————————— 25,00
I Ladies riding habit,—————————————————————— I5,00
2 Wool dresses,————————————————————————— I5,00
I Evening dress,————————————————————————— 25,00
Ladies under wear,————————————————————————— 20,00
2 Wash dresses,—————————————————————————— 4,00
I Suit men's clothing,———————————————————— 75,00
I Beaver vest,————————————————————————————— I5,00
2 Buffalo over coats,———————————————————————— 50,00
I Canvass over coat,————————————————————————— I2,00
I Cloth over coat,——————————————————————————— I8,00
8 Over skirts,————————————————————————————— 24,00
3 Suits Lisle under wear,———————————————————— 30,00
2 Suits camel's hair,——————————————————————— I8,00
4 Suits flannel,——————————————————————————— 32,00
4 Suits of Balbrigan,————————————————————————— 00,00
Under wear,————————————————————————————— 40,00
2 Suits clothes,——————————————————————————— 50,00

3 Hats,	$ 24,00
2 valises,	12,00
300 rounds cartridges,	5,00
I half dozen Lisle thread socks,	6,00
I dozen pair cotton socks,	6,00
3 dozen pair Dutch socks,	15,00
3 dozen pair of over shoes,	7,50
12 White shirts,	36,00
I Cross cut saw,	5,50
I Handle cross cut saw,	4,50
2 Drawing knives,	2,50
2 Smoothing planes,	3,00
I Jack plane,	I,25
2 Broad axes,	7,00
I Brace,	3,00
I half dozen bits,	I,75
2 Augurs $I,50—Grind stone and fixtures, $300,	4,50
2 Hand saws,	5,50
2 Axes, $3,80, and 2 chisels $1,00	4,80
I Dwelling house,	2500,00
I Stable,	500,00
2 Corrals,	80,00
I McCormick's reaper,	100,00
I Hay rake,	25,00
3 Sets harness, damages,	28,50
I Cheyenne Collins saddle,	50,00 ✓
I Double sized Texas saddle,	45,00
10 Tons of hay,	100,00
5 Pitch forks,	6,25
I Hay knife,	3,50
I Side saddle,	27,00
I Pair leather leggins,	10,00
I Pair leather leggins,	12,00 ✓
2 Shears, $6, Tent and pole $7,50	13,50
I Wall tent and pole, $10,00	
2 Wagon sheets, $10,00	20,00 ✓
I Shot gun (breech loading),	30,00
I Marlin Repeating Rifle,	35,00
500 lbs. Bacon at 14 cts.,	70,00
Flour, at $4,50	22,50
120 pounds Arbucle coffee,	30,00
100 pounds of sugar,	15,70
15 pounds of tea,	13,50
20 pounds of Hominy,	I,40

10 pounds of rice, —————————————————————————$ 1,10
40 pounds of beans at 47 and a half cts. per lb.—   3,00
3 Cases Tomatoes at $4, per case, ——————————————   12,00
10 lbs. oat meal at 8cts. per lb.——————————————   ,80
15 pounds dried corn at 12 and a half cts.—————   1,87 1/2

17 pounds Baking powder at 45 cts.————————————   7,65
10 cured venison hams, ——————————————————————   7,50
8 pounds canned Salmon at 40cts.————————————   2,40
8 pounds canned beef, ——————————————————————   2,40
1 Box of crackers, 10 lbs at 40 cts.——————————   4,00
10 lbs. of plum butter at 10cts.——————————————   1,00
3 pounds of jelly at 35 cts.——————————————————   1,05
10 pounds Pickle at 10 cts.———————————————————   1,00
1 Kit mackerel, —————————————————————————————   2,25
10 lbs. cod fish, ———————————————————————————   1,25
1 Box of soap, ——————————————————————————————   7,50
20 pounds of corn starch, ———————————————————   2,50
4 bottles Extract of Vanilla, ———————————————   ,50
50 pounds table salt, ———————————————————————   1,50
23 Chickens, ————————————————————————————————   23,00
1 Cooking stove and fixtures, ————————————————   50,00
1 Extension table, ——————————————————————————   9,00
1 doz. chairs, ——————————————————————————————   10,00
1 set of dishes, ————————————————————————————   17,00
1 kitchen table, ————————————————————————————   5,00
1 dozen milk pans, —————————————————————————   4,80
2 doz.solid silver tea spoons at $18, ———————   36,00
1 half doz. table spoons solid silver, ——————   15,00
1 half dozen plated table spoons, ———————————   5,00
1 dinner castor, ————————————————————————————   10,00
2 silver plated pickle castors, ————————————   7,00
2 solid silver sugar spoons, —————————————————   8,00
1 solid silver berry spoon, ——————————————————   8,00
1 solid silver ladle, ———————————————————————   10,00
1 dozen plated knives, ——————————————————————   5,00
1 dozen plated forks, ———————————————————————   10,00
2 solid silver candle sticks, ———————————————   50,00
1 silver plated napkin ring, —————————————————   1,50
1 solid silver butter knife, —————————————————   2,50
1 plated butter knife, ——————————————————————   ,75
1 plated silver butter dish, —————————————————   4,00
1 plated silver cake basket, —————————————————   4,00
1 gold ring, ————————————————————————————————   8,00
1 pair ear rings, ———————————————————————————   8,00

I Gold cross, ——————————————————————$ 25,00
3 silver plated mugs, ———————————————— 6,00
I hand painted tete-a-tete, set, ———————————— 10,00
I Gold watch and chain, ————————————————I50,00
I Necklace, ——————————————————————— 25,00
I Shaving case, ———————————————————— 7,00
I Brush and comb case, with mirror, ————————— I5,00
In addition to this list, Zook, in his petition adds
the following:-
I pair shoes , new, ———————————————————— 10,00
I pair shoes, —————————————————————— 6,00
6 Flannel shirts, —————————————————————I8,00
4 Suits of underclothes, ——————————————— 20,00
To the above should be added the following amounts
claimed in the joint application of claimants.
For freight of goods from Miles city, Custer County,
Montana, at $I,25 per I00 lbs. amounting, to———— 70,00
To damages to business of said firm, by said depre-
dation, ———————————————————————————I000,00

Total, ——————————————$6875, 47I/2

The above amount is compiled, from the statements contained,
in the separate and joint petitions of the claimants, and the
schedule of the lost property, which is referred to in the said
petitions, and attached to the same, and which correctly added
foots up the sum of $ 6875, 47I/2 . Claimants acknowledge, the
recovery of the following named articles, which should be deducted from the above aggregate, in order to obtain, the actual
amount of claimants account, for which they ask indemnity.

I Cheyenne Collins saddle, ——————————————$ 50,00
I Pair leather leggins, ————————————————— I2,00
I Wall tent, ——————————————————————— I0,00
2 Wagon sheets, ————————————————————— I0,00
40 Pounds bacon, ————————————————————— 5,60

50 Pounds of flour, ————————————————————$ 2,25
25 Pounds of Arbucle coffee, ———————————————   6,25
20 Pounds of sugar, ———————————————————   3,14

(The above article is erroneously carried out by claimants, at $2,10—In the schedule of lost property—
  100 lbs. of sugar is set down, at $15,70—20 lbs.be-
  ing one fifth,at the same price charged,would be
  $3,14———————————————————————————————)

I Kit of Mackerel, ———————————————————   2,25
10 Pounds of soap, ————————————————————   1,30
I Writing desk damaged, ————————————————   10,00
2 Pairs of pillow cases, ——————————————————   1,25
I Pair of pillows, ———————————————————   6,00
5 and a half blankets, ——————————————————   72,50
I Marseilles bedspread, ———————————————————   6,00
I Bear robe, ——————————————————————   15,00
I Buffalo robe, —————————————————————   10,00
I Mountain lion robe, ———————————————————   10,00
2 Bear skins, —————————————————————   9,00
Ladies underwear, ————————————————————   5,00
I Buffalo over-coat, ————————————————————   25,00
I Cloth over-coat, ————————————————————   18,00
I Over skirt, ———————————————————————   3,00
I Suit Lisle thread underwear, —————————————   10,00
I Hat, —————————————————————————   8,00
2 Valises, ——————————————————————   12,00
4 White shirts, —————————————————————   12,00
I Gold watch and chain, ———————————————   150,00
I Necklace, —————————————————————   25,00
2 Drawing knives, ————————————————————   2,50

(The above in claimants original account, is charged at $2,50 and in crediting the return, should
  be for same amount,instead of $4,50 as entered on-
  claimants list of returned property.———————————)

2 Smoothing planes, —————————————————   3,00
I Shaving case, ——————————————————————   7,00
I Brush and comb case with mirror, ——————————   15,00
                                                   ————————
                                                   $538,04

Which last named sum deducted from claimants original amount

leaves claimants actual claim,of indemnity,asked,for $6337,

four and one half cents.

In support of said claim,Nannie T. Aldersan, the wife of one of said firm,duly executed her deposition,on the 25th day of April,1884,which is in substance as follows:—

"That she is the wife of W. W. Aldersan,one of the firm of Zook & Aldersan,who are claimants,for the loss of property on "Lame Deer Creek,"in the County of Custer,Montana Territory,that she was familiar with the improvements,house hold furniture,tools,implements,provisions,which are set forth in the schedule hereto attached.That the goods and chattels therein mentioned,were in use in,and a bout the premises described in claimants,petitions,and were of value stated in said schedule.That she has no knowledge of the recovery of any of the said articles,except as stated in the foregoing schedule."

Brown Taliafero,of Custer County,Montana,being duly sworn ,April 23rd,1884,in substance says:—"That he has heard read the petition of claimant Walter W. Aldersan,and knows the contents thereof,and that the statements contained in said petition,he knows of his own knowledge to be true, That said depredation,was committed within his observation, and was done with force of arms."

Charles Rineheart,of Custer County,Montana,being duly sworn April 25th,1884,in substance says:—"That on or about

the 18th of March, 1884, he was employed by claimants, upon
their premises, on "Lame Deer Creek", Montana, that on said day,
the improvemens and property of claimants, on said premises,
were destroyed or carried away, by Cheyenne Indians, under the
leadership of "Black Wolf", That after the Indians had taken
possession of said premises, he and one Brown Taliafero, came
in sight of the house and premises, while the Indians were
burning and destroying the same, that the Indians resisted
affiant, and said Taliafero's, approach to the premises, and
that said Indians, destroyed and carried away all of the property about the same."

Walrond S. Snell, being duly sworn, April 3rd, 1884, in substance says:-"He resided in Miles City, Custer County, Montana,
his occupation, a merchant, wholesale and retail dealer, in furniture. That he made the list of articles hereto attached, and
affixed opposite each item, the actual weight of same, desig-
nating the number of pounds, and weight of each."

Attached to said deposition, is a schedule of articles
claimed to be lost and the weight of each given, the whole
number of articles lost, being put down at 5,654 pounds, as
their weight.

W. S. Dyer, late the U. S. Indian Agent, in charge of the
Cheyenne Indians, in Montana, to whom the claim was referred

for investigation, and report, under date of May 19th, 1884, in substance says :-"That he was in charge of said Indians, when the depredation was committed, and that he is personally acquainted with the witnesses, and considers them all reliable, that witness Snell, he considers to be one of the best men in Miles City, that he has examined the prices charged and considers them fair and just. He is personnally acquainted with the claimants, and also with the ranch, having spent several days there, previous to the depredation, and thinks that claimants could not replace the buildings burned for the sum charged, that claimants ranch, was the finest in the country.

Most of the articles lost he has seen, but cannot swear to the amount; but knows the quantity was large and the quality good. That a large portion of the silver ware were wedding presents, a little more than a year before they were stolen. That it was impossible to hold a council with the Indians, as "Black Wolf" and his band, were a remnant of the Indians at Red Cloud Agency, and away from the Agency more than a year, and from the further fact, they were in jail at Miles' City. That to his personal knowledge, neither one of the claimants are to be blamed, for the loss."

On May 28th, 1887, R.L. Upshaw, U.S. Indian Agent, at Tongue River, Agency, Montana Territory, made his report to this

office,in substance as follows:-"Having submitted this claim
to the Cheyenne Indians of this Agency,and taken testimony
of such persons as I thought best informed on the subject,I
have the honor to submit the following:-The Indians say the
houses of the claimants were burned with the contents,by members of the tribe,but that four of the tribe,"Howling Wolf,"
"White Bear,""Stand Aside,"and "Handle,"were tried and con-
victed of the offense, Howling Wolf" pleading guilty,and
sent to the Penitentiary.—"Handle",died,and the others were
pardoned by the President.That the balance of the tribe had
nothing to do with it,and are not responsible and the pun-
ishment inflicted should settle the matter,so far as they are
concerned.

The council also ask that the accompanying statement,
of "Black Wolf",should be forwarded,I forward also a number
of affidavits,as to credibility of partners and witnesses."

The statement of "Black Wolf,"referred to in the prece-
ding report,is in substance as follows:-"The claimants,had
two men at work for them,I visited the house,and one of the
men,a young man,gave me dinner,and tobacco,after dinner I was
smoking a cigar,and the man was dancing and playing Indian
around me,and while at my back,I received a shot on the head
and fell unconscious from the chair. As soon as I became

conscious,I got up and walked to the mouth of the "Lame
Deer Creek,"about three miles,and reached there about sun-
down.As soon as my relations saw me,they became excited and
went and burned the house.Four of them "Howling Wolf,""White
Bear",Stands Aside," and Handle,"were arrested,tried,and
sent to the Penitentiary,"Handle died,and the other three
were pardoned,after serving twelve months and three days in
the Penitentiary.I did not know the man who shot me it was
my first visit to the house,The man who shot me ran away."

Accompanying the said report, are the affidavits of Walter
R. Jordan,Wm. Green,J. T. Robinson,and E. R. Brown, who
swear to the standing and credibility of claimants and witnesses.

On December 4th,1884,this office made its report upon
the claim to the Department,recommending its allowance for
the sum of $ 4739,83————said report was forwarded by the
Department to Congress,and by Act of that body,approved Mar.
3rd,1885,the claim was returned to this office,for re-ex-
amination,and report,in conformity to said act.The foregoing
comprises a full history of all action had on the claim,with
a liberal abstract of all testimony pertaining to same.

The amount for which claimants ask an indemnity,after
deducting from their original account,the amount of property

which they recovered is, the sum of $6337,041/. In this amount

2

there are included two items, one for freight in hauling goods
from Miles City, $70,00 and one for general damage to the
business of the firm, amounting to $1000, the two items making
up the sum of $1070, . It is submitted that these items, under
the law regulating the adjustment of claims of this character, are not legitimate demands, and should therefore, be struck
from claimants account. The charge of $1000, is purely spec-
ulative, whilst the law in cases of this character, only author
-izes compensating damages, and not vindictive damages, and
most certainly where the claim in addition shows it to be
not simply consequential, but also speculative, in its character, such opinion has been uniformly adhered to, since the or-
ganization of this office, With respect to the item of $70,00
for the hauling of the goods from Miles City, it is conceded,
that under circumstances which show, that it should be added a
as a part of the cost or value of the goods, at the place
where stolen; such demand would be legitimate, but in this case
such circumstances are not disclosed by the testimony.

The claimants make out first, a schedule of the property
lost, and affix to it a value, and then propose to add the
price of the freight, thereby making a double charge for the
same item. In the form presented, such item must be rejected.

With the above indicated items, deducted from claimants general account, there would remain the sum of $5287,04I/2 as the legitimate demand of claimants.

In the opinion of this office, the depredation as charged in the petitions, was committed and that claimants lost the property enumerated therein. The testimony of the witnesses is direct, and from personal observation. It must be remarked however, that under the testimony, this office cannot accept of the estimate of value, made by the claimants of the lost property. No such description of the lost property is given, as will enable the adjuster to determine the correctness of such estimate, and it would seem from an examination of the account, that a majority of the articles are given a value beyond the original cost of them, when new, whilst the evidence and facts show, the articles were second hand and had been in use for over one year, and had been subjected to the casualties of being transported quite a distance. Under such a state of circumstances, it is believed, that a reduction of 25 per cent, upon the amount of claimants demand, when reduced as aforesaid, to the sum of $5287,04I/2, would give a fair compensation for the property lost, making the value of the property lost, as estimated by this office the sum of $3950,28.

In accordance with such views, this office, now submits its formal conclusions upon the claim, as follows:—

Ist.—That claimants were citizens of the U. S. at the time of the alleged depredation.

2nd.—That a band of Northern Cheyenne Indians,in Custer County,Montana Territory,on the I8th day of March,I884,com- mitted a depredation upon the property of claimants,whereby claimants lost property of the value of $3950,28 and in such loss,neither the claimants nor the employes,are chargeable with contributory negligence.

3rd.—That the tribe of Northern Cheyenne Indians,at the date of said injury,was in treaty relations with the U.S. proclaimed August 25th,I868,and by Art.I of said treaty , said injury is chargeable against said tribe,vide I9 Stat. 256——I5 Stat.655.

4th.—This office recommends an allowance of $3950,28 in full satisfaction of said claim:

Very Respectfully

L S C Atkins

Commissioner

Bell

BIBLIOGRAPHY

MANUSCRIPTS

National Archives

United States Court of Claims: Indian Depredations, Case #4688
(Zook and Alderson vs the United States and the Cheyenne Indians),
Record Group 123.
United States Court of Claims, Department of Justice: Indian
Depredations, Case #4688 (Zook and Alderson Vs the United States
and the Cheyenne Indians), 1884, RG 205.

State Historical Society of North Dakota

Huidekoper, A.C., "My Experiences and Investment in the Bad Lands
of North Dakota and Some of the Men I met There."

Lindsay, Mrs. W. M., "My Pioneer Years in North Dakota."

Longfellow, Daniel W., "Papers."

Stoddard, John B., "Business Papers."

Billings County Court House

Deed Book "A" of Billings County in court house, Medora, North Dakota.

National Park Service

Johnson, Sally, "Maltese Cross Cabin: Reconstruction and Furnishing
Plan," 1960, in Museum Branch Files, Washington.

Mattison, Ray H., "Interpretive Planning Report on Longhorn Ranch
Project, Peaceful Valley, Theodore Roosevelt National Memorial
Park," February 1961, in Division of History Files, OAHP, Washington.

Rickey, Don, Jr., "Cowboy Dress, Arms, Tools, and Equipment as used
in the Little Missouri Range Country and the Medora Area in the
1880s," 1957, in Division of History Files, OAHP, Washington.

Taylor, Dee C., "Archeological Investigations of the Elkhorn Ranch
Site," 1962, in Division of History Files, OAHP, Washington.

Theodore Roosevelt National Memorial Park

"Old Timers File" in Park Interpreters Office.

NEWSPAPERS

Bismarch *Tribune*, September 7, 1883-February 27, 1885.

The Dickenson *Press*, March 31, 1883-February 29, 1896.

The Bad Lands Cow Boy (Medora), February 7, 1884-December 23, 1886.

PERSONAL INTERVIEWS

Hubbard, Dr. Ralph, Personal Interview, September 26, 1969, by Lenard E. Brown and Alfred Schulmeyer, Park Historian, Medora, North Dakota.

Prior, O. Walter, Personal Interview, June 26, 1966, by Lindon F. Wood, Medora, North Dakota.

BOOKS AND MAGAZINES

Alderson, Nannie T., and Helen H. Smith, *A Bride Goes West*, New York, Farrar and Rinehart, 1942.

Armstrong, James B., *The Big North*, Missoula, University of Montana, 1965.

Banks, Charles E. and L. Armstrong, *Theodore Roosevelt: A Typical American*, Chicago, Du Mont, 1901.

Beitz, Lester V., *Treasury of Frontier Relics*, New York, Edwin House, 1966.

Briggs, Harold E., *Frontiers of The Northwest: A History of The Upper Missouri Valley*, New York, Appleton-Century Co., 1940.

Brooks, Chester and R. Mattison, *Theodore Roosevelt and the Dakota Badlands*, Washington, G.P.O., 1958.

Brown, Dee, and Martin Schmitt, *Trail Driving Days*, New York, Scribners, 1952.

Brown, Mark H., and W. R. Felton, *Before Barbed Wire: L. A. Huffman, Photographer on Horseback*, Henry Holt and Company, 1956.

Cowles, Anna Roosevelt, *Letters From Theodore Roosevelt to Anna Roosevelt Cowles, 1870-1918*,

Crawford, Lewis F., *Badlands and Broncho Trails*, Bismarck Capital Book Company, 1922.

Hagedorn, Hermann, *Roosevelt in the Badlands*, New York, Houghton Mifflin Company, 1921.

Hagen, Olaf T., and R. Mattison, "Pyramid Park: Where Roosevelt Came to Hunt," *North Dakota History*, Vol. 19 (October 1952), pp. 1-27.

Hamilton, W. H., "Dakota: An Autobiography of a Cowman," *South Dakota Historical Collections*, Vol. 19, 1938.

Huidekoper, Wallis, *The Land of the Dakotas*, Helena, Montana Stockgrowers Association, no date.

Johnston, Harry V., *My Home on The Range: Frontier Life in The Badlands*, St. Paul, The Webb Publishing Co., 1942.

Kuhn, Bertha M., "The W-Bar Ranch on The Missouri Slope," *Collections of State Historical Society of North Dakota*, Vol. 5 (Grand Forks, 1923), pp. 155-66.

Lang, Lincoln A, *Ranching With Roosevelt*, Philadelphia, Lippincott, 1926.

Lodge, Henry C., *Selections From The Correspondence of Theodore Roosevelt and Henry Cabot Lodge* (2 vols), New York, Scribners, 1925.

Mattison, Ray H., "Life at Roosevelt's Elkhorn Ranch--The Letters of William W. and Mary Sewall," *North Dakota History*, Vol. 27 (Summer and Fall, 1960), pp. 105-43.

Morrison, Elting E. (ed), *The Letters of Theodore Roosevelt* (8 vols), Cambridge, Harvard University Press, 1951.

Pelissier, Kate Roberts, "Reminiscences of a Pioneer Mother," *North Dakota History*, Vol. 24 (July 1957), pp. 129-39.

The Phonograph and How To Use It, National Phonograph Company, 1900.

Putnam, Carleton, *Theodore Roosevelt: The Formative Years, 1858-1886,* New York, Scribner's, 1958.

Randall, Isabelle, *A Lady's Ranche Life in Montana,* London, W. H. Allen & Co., 1887.

Roberts, T. F., "Pioneer Life in Western North Dakota," *North Dakota History,* Vol. 15 (1948), pp. 153-69, 225-65.

Robinson, Corinne Roosevelt, *My Brother Theodore Roosevelt,* New York, Scribners, 1921.

Robinson, Elwyn B., *History of North Dakota,* Lincoln, University of Nebraska Press, 1966.

Roosevelt, Theodore, *Theodore Roosevelt: An Autobiography,* New York, MacMillan, 1919.

Roosevelt, Theodore, *Hunting Trips of a Ranchman* in *The Works of Theodore Roosevelt,* H. Hagedorn (Ed), Vol 1 (20 volumes), New York, Scribners, 1926.

Roosevelt, T., *The Wilderness Hunter* in *The Works of Theodore Roosevelt,* H. Hagedorn (Ed), Vol. 2 (20 volumes), New York, Scribners, 1926.

Sewall, William W., *Will Sewall's Story of T. R.,* New York, Harpers, 1919.

Stickney, V. H., "The Roundup," *North Dakota Historical Quarterly,* Vol. 1 (October 1926), pp. 3-16.

Steinbeck, John, *Travels With Charley,* New York, Viking Press, 1962.

Stuart, Granville, *Forty Years on The Frontier,* 2 volumes, Cleveland, Arthur H. Clark, 1925.

Welsh, Donald H., "Pierre Wibaux, Cattle King," *North Dakota History,* Vol. 20 (January, 1953), pp. 5-25.

ILLUSTRATIONS

1. Old OX Ranch House near Marmarth, N. D.

The old OX Ranch House near Marmarth, North Dakota, forty miles southwest of Medora was built in 1883. The OX was a large Texas ranch. Mark H. Brown and W. R. Felton, *Before Barbed Wire: L. A. Huffman, Photographer on Horseback* (New York, 1956), p. 45. Cited hereafter as Brown and Felton, *Before Barbed Wire*.

2. Deacon Wade Ranch House in 1961

Deacon Wade was a contemporary of Roosevelt in the Badlands. Mrs. Wade never quite accepted the mores of the West thus causing herself and others much anguish. This photograph and the previous one illustrate the simple design and materials of ranches along the Little Missouri River.

Photograph of the "Deacon" Wade ranch home built in the 1880's, located about 12 miles south of Sedona. The portion in the foreground is a part of the original structure. (Photo by Richard Meador, February 1967.)

3. Interior of an Old Time Ranch on the Powder River

This photograph by Huffman, though undated, is indicative of the furnishings of a ranch kitchen-dining room. Note the bread rising in the dishpan beside the stove, the cooking utensils hung from nails or pegs, the shelf, work table, chairs and bench, food safe with banjo case on top, and carbine and pistol. Brown and Felton, *Before Barbed Wire*, p. 46.

Interior of an Old Time Hotel, Powder River.

4. Interior of a Line Camp Cabin

L. A. Huffman, whose photographic record of the North Plains covers the year 1878 to 1905, had his office in Miles City, Montana. He took this interior of a line camp cabin probably during the 1880's. The stencil CROW AG -- indicates that this may have been a ranch with a lease to run cattle on the reservation southeast of Billings. Note the coffee pot and kettle on the stove, the homemade chair, and items hanging on the wall. Brown and Felton, *Before Barbed Wire*, p. 42.

5. Ranch House Near Henry's Lake in Idaho, 1872

Though a bit early for our study, this is included for the collection of firearms above and beside the mantle as well as the cooking utensils. Clarence Jackson, *The Look of the Old West* (New York, 1947), p. 168.

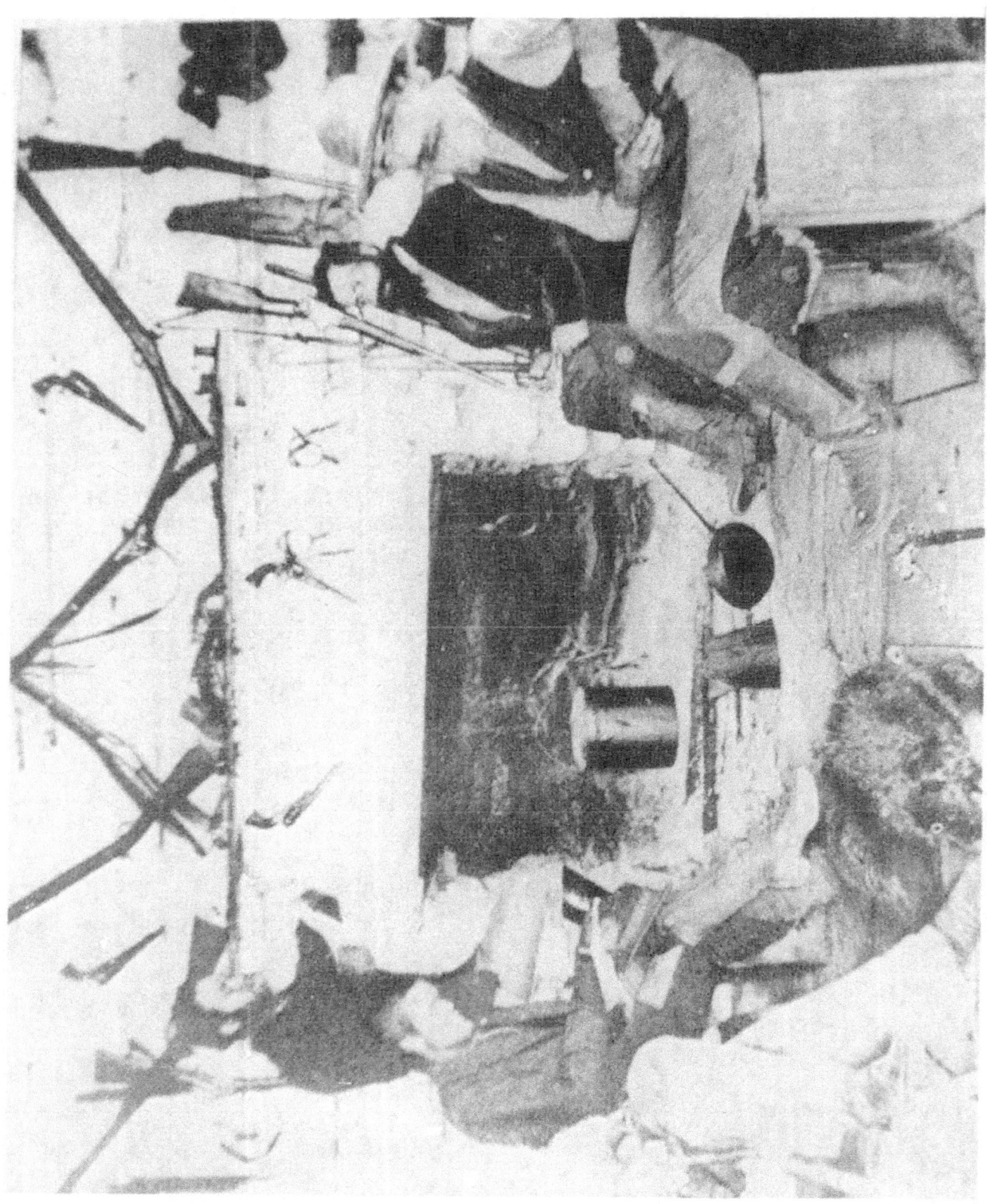

6. A Group of Roosevelt's Badlands Contemporaries

Hagedorn in *Roosevelt in the Badlands*, page 176, described this as "A Group of Bad Lands Citizens." The ranch house in the background may be A. C. Huidekoper's. The men have been identified as follows: Front row seated-- T.F. Roberts, Norman Lebo, A. C. Huidekoper, Hell Roaring Bill Jones, George Woodman, and McQuilken. Standing--Goose (Crow Indian), Charles Mason, Charles Van Sickle, Herman Holst, Jim Harmon, Don Fowler, Fred McClain, James Reynolds, and Schuyler Lebo. Nearly all were in the Little Missouri region with Roosevelt. The various styles of chairs shown reflect some types found in ranches of the era.

7. Rocking Chairs on the Elkhorn Piazza

The piazza at the Elkhorn ranch was photographed by Theodore Roosevelt. The number of elk horns bears out its name. Two of Roosevelt's favorite chairs sit on the porch and a saddle with rifle scabbard, and a belt and holster are on the right in the photograph. Hagedorn, *Roosevelt in the Bad Lands*, p. 370.

8. XIT Cook Mexican John Baking Pies on a Montana Roundup

The XIT was another Texas outfit. The items shown here on the drop leaf of the chuck wagon would also be common to the kitchen of a Montana ranch in the 1880s or 1890s. Dee Brown and Martin Schmidt, *Trail Driving Days* (New York, 1952), p. 199.

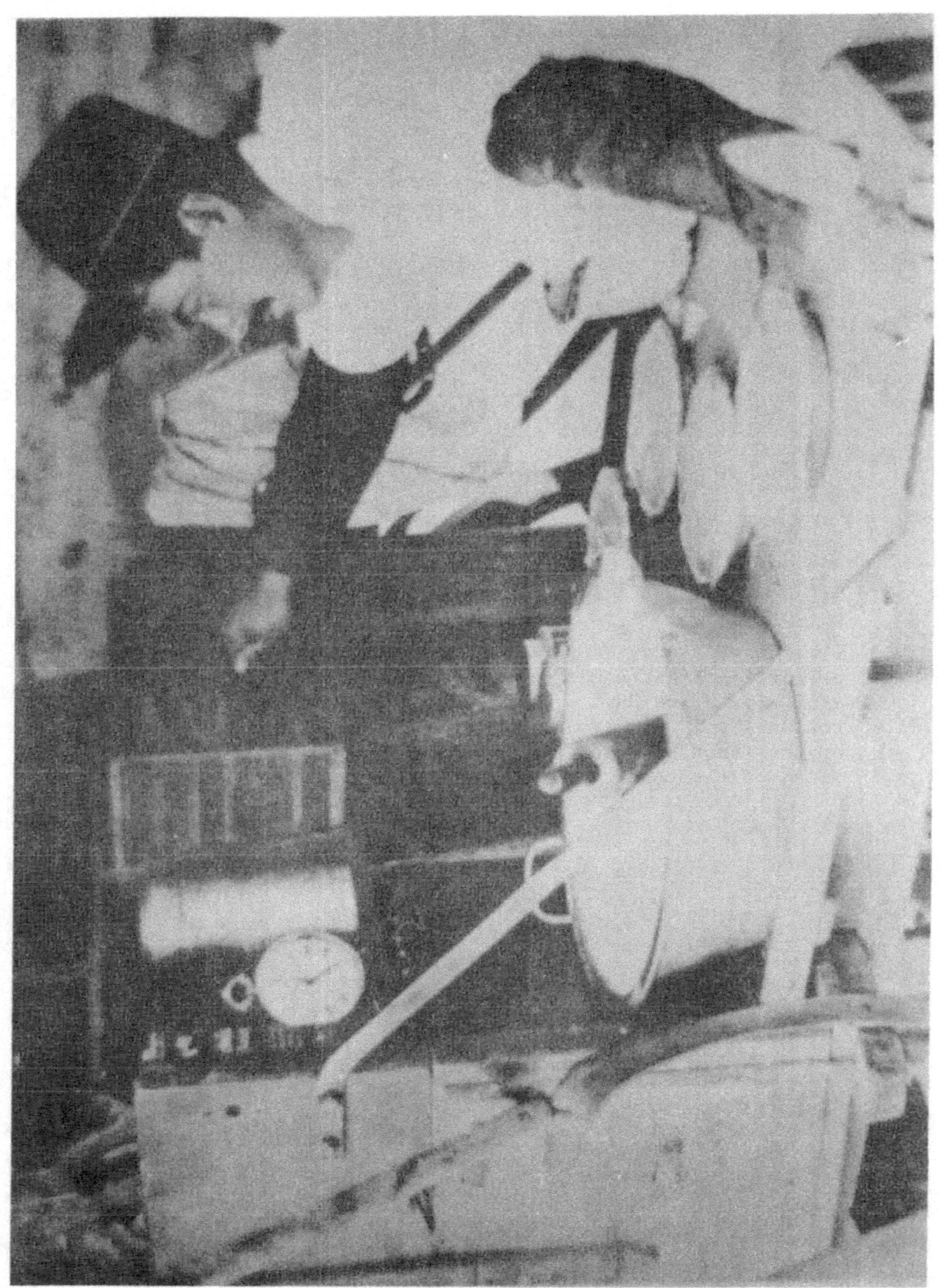

9. A Food Safe and Jars Used in Home Canning

Both these illustrations are from Lester V. Beitz, *Treasury of Frontier Relics*. The food safe with its perforated front and side panels was used to store items for a few days. The types of jars "from Mrs. Soddy's cellar shelf" are typical of what would have been used by the ranch wife for home canning during the last twenty years of the century.

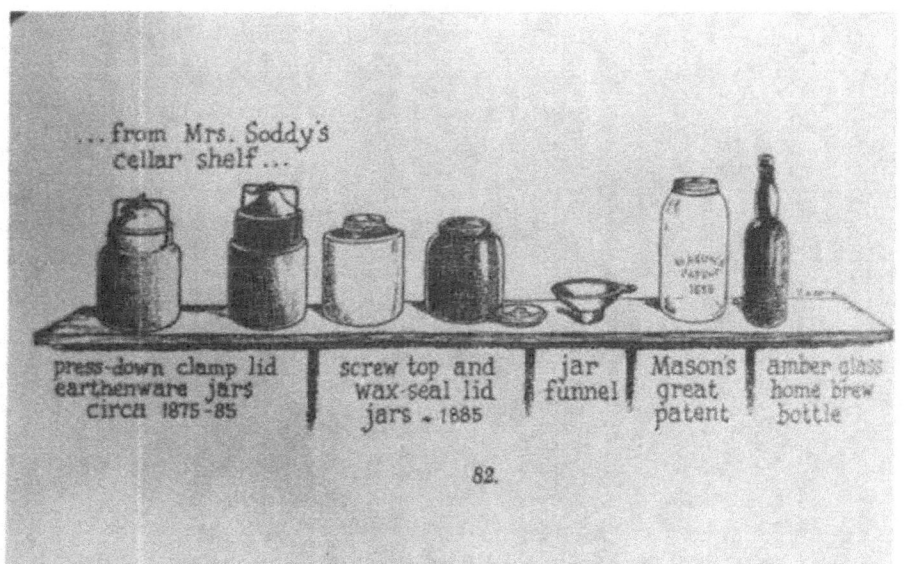

...from Mrs. Soddy's
cellar shelf...

| press-down clamp lid earthenware jars circa 1875-85 | screw top and wax-seal lid jars - 1885 | jar funnel | Mason's great patent | amber glass home brew bottle |

82.

10. Two Other Frontier Relics

In *Treasury of Frontier Relics*, pages 28-30,
Lester Beitz describes the tub-shaped pot that was a
cast-iron dutch oven. In the hands of a good roundup
cook it would provide the best food a hungry cowboy
ever ate. Coals were heaped on top of the lid as well
as below and around the base. In the ranch kitchen
the dutch oven also was used either in the cookstove's
oven or at the fireplace.

Dad purchased Union Leader, if that was his choice
for a chew, in tin boxes such as this. When the boxes
were empty, the children would carry them to school as
lunch pails. Beitz, *Treasury of Frontier Relics*,
p. 231.

11. Tidy Rack and Angle Lamp

The tidy rack hung near the washstand in many ranch houses. A mirror fit into the half-circle at the top, the tray held a comb or other items, and the two rings would hold towels. Beitz gave the following measurements for the one pictured: 19 inches high, 11 inches wide, and 5/8 inch thick. Made of solid oak, it weighed nearly four pounds.

The Angle Lamp was discussed in the text. This model was attached to the wall and sold for $1.80 during the late 1880s and 1890s.

Illustrations from Beitz, *Treasury of Frontier Relics*, pp. 124 and 182.

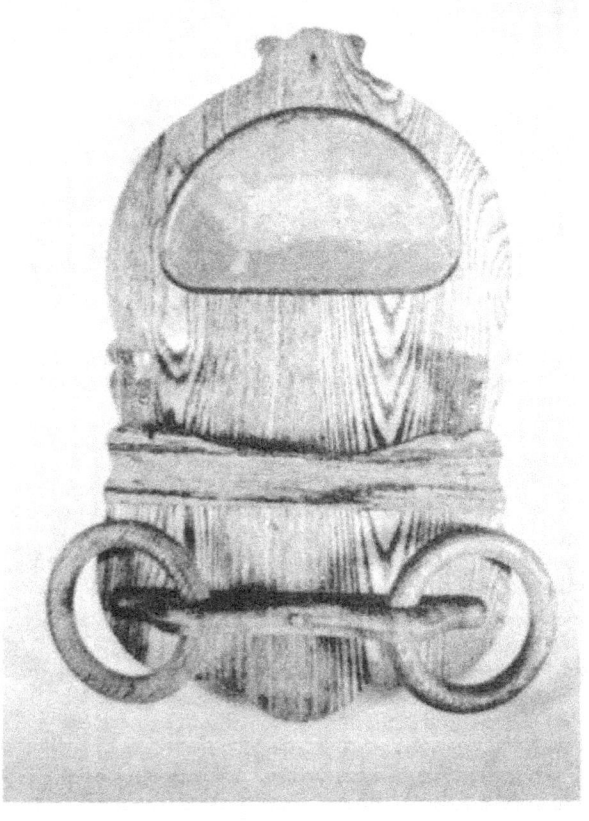

12. Heating and Cooking Stoves

Two advertisements from the Dickenson *Press* showing the type of cooking and heating stoves being sold in North Dakota in 1883-84.

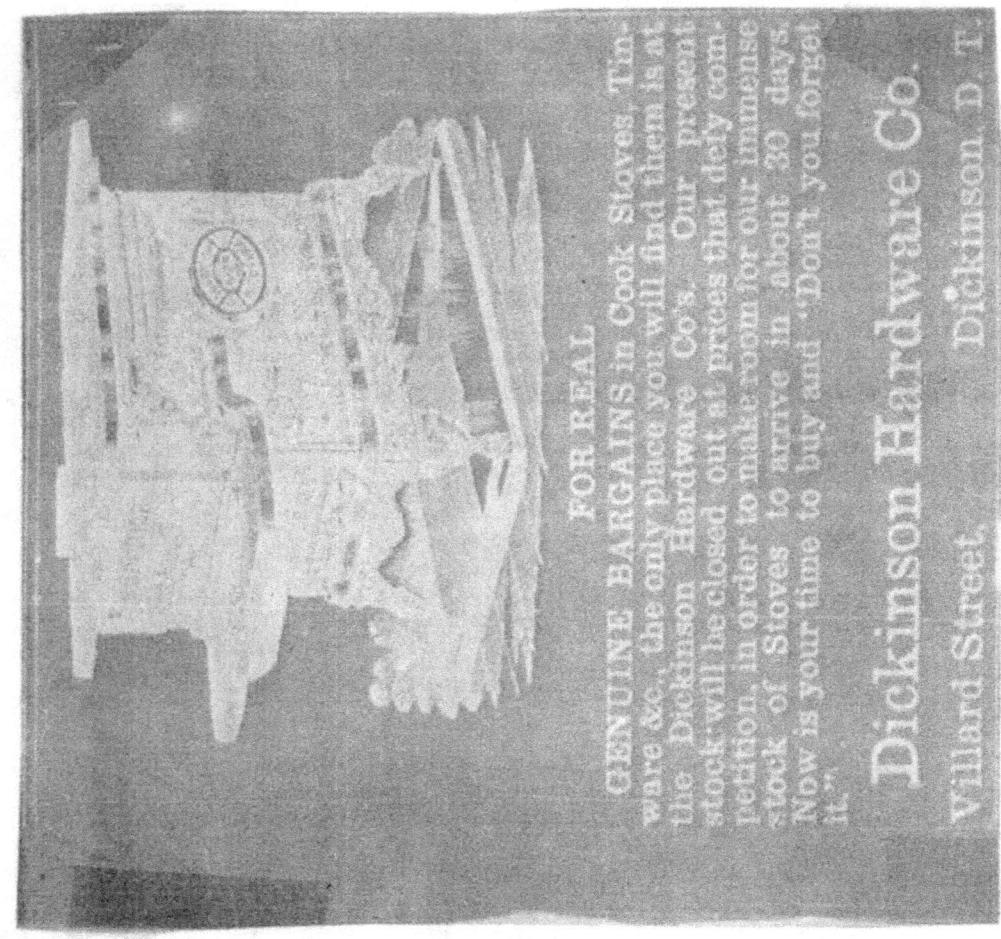

FOR REAL
GENUINE BARGAINS in Cook Stoves. Tinware &c., the only place you will find them is at the Dickinson Hardware Co's. Our present stock will be closed out at prices that defy competition in order to make room for our immense stock of Stoves to arrive in about 30 days. Now is your time to buy and "Don't you forget it."

Dickinson Hardware Co.

Villard Street,   Dickinson, D. T.

THE DICKINSON PRESS, March 15, 1884

CATCH ON
quick to one of those elegant Heating or Cook Stoves at the Dickinson Hardware Co. They are going off rapidly, and now is the time to buy, before the assortment is broken. Every one guaranteed to burn the Lignite Coal with the very best results. Don't fail to see them.

Dickinson Hardware Co.

Villard Street,   Dickinson, D. T.

THE DICKINSON PRESS, October 13, 1883